CW00504783

Life in Victorian Bristol

Life in
Victorian Bristol

Helen Reid

redcliffe

First published in 2005 by Redcliffe Press Ltd.,
81g Pembroke Road, Bristol BS8 3EA

© Helen Reid 2005
ISBN–10 1 904537 40 5
ISBN–13 978 1 904537 40 3

British Library Cataloguing-in-Publication Data
A catalogue record for this book is available from the British Library

All rights reserved. Except for the purpose of review, no part of this book may be
reproduced, stored in a retrieval system, or transmitted, in any form or by any means,
electronic, mechanical, photocopying, recording or otherwise, without the
prior permission of the publishers.

Design and typesetting by Stephen Morris smc@freeuk.com
Printed in Malta by the Gutenberg Press Ltd.

Contents

Victorian Bristol's waterfront.

Introduction

Bristol is often thought of as medieval and Georgian but the core of the modern city is Victorian.

The infrastructure of modern Bristol was laid down in the nineteenth century, with the system of local government, road and rail layouts, and siting of the business quarter. The Victorians set up all the institutions we take for granted in a modern city: the police force, the fire brigade, the post office, telephones, sewerage, lighting, refuse collection, gas and electricity, water. They built the schools, the libraries, the swimming baths, their leading citizens put up the money for the city's art gallery and other institutions – and if you removed the Victorian contribution from Bristol, the place would be a backwater.

Queen Victoria herself visited the city only twice: once in 1830 as Princess Victoria, aged 11, when she visited with her mother the Duchess of Kent, and stayed in a first-floor suite at the Clifton Hotel in The Mall, and again right at the end of her reign, in 1899, when she was 80. Between those two dates, Bristol changed radically, stamped by the new Victorian ethos.

What was it like to live in this age of progress and industry, of self-improvement and selective charity? Through extracts from books, letters, journals and newspapers, this book is an attempt to convey the flavour of Victorian Bristol and describe the social and economic systems which made the city function.

We feel we can understand the Victorians, perhaps because photography was invented two years into Victoria's reign. We know what Victorian Bristol and its inhabitants looked like, we still live in the houses they built, we shop at the firms they founded, drink in the pubs they drank in, drive on roads they built. So were they so different from us?

Broad Street, Bristol, engraving from John Britton's *Bath and Bristol, with the Counties of Somerset and Gloucester: A Series of Views*, 1829.

1 Prologue: 1837

A KEY EVENT that was to influence Bristol's future prosperity happened in 1837, the year Queen Victoria came to the throne: Brunel's *Great Western*, the first ever transatlantic steamship, was launched from William Patterson's shipyards at Wapping Wharf on July 19, before a crowd of 50,000. The revolutionary ship, which weighed 1,340 tons and cost the owners £63,000, was to be Bristol's new link with North America, and a contract to deliver the transatlantic mail had been negotiated.

With visionary foresight, Brunel also planned an integrated transport system: his passengers would come via the Great Western Railway from London to Temple Meads station, stay overnight at the Royal Western Hotel (now Brunel House) and then would embark on the steamship for New York. Brunel's railway had by then reached Taplow and Box Tunnel was being dug out. In 1837, Daniel Gooch was appointed as locomotive superintendent and the first locomotive arrived in November. It was to be the start of Bristol's great new transport era.

The *Great Western* made the first run to New York the following year, and returned to Bristol with 66 passengers and 20,000 letters in a record 12 days 14 hours, cutting a day off the time it took to travel from Liverpool. But, as always, Bristol was slow to take advantage of its lead; the backers delayed a decision on building more steamships, and concentrated on building an even larger one, the *Great Britain*. The Merchant Venturers, who owned the docks, refused to lower the dues, and Liverpool began to win more trade.

And though Brunel had put Bristol on the map with his famous steamships, the *Great Western* and the *Great Britain* that followed in 1843, this actually sowed the seeds of the port's decline: Bristol's locks were too narrow for the big ships and the passage down the tidal Avon was too difficult and dangerous for the new breed of big ships to navigate.

In 1837 Bristol was still recovering from the effects of the violent riots of 1831, digesting the results of the Reform Bill and, more importantly, the Municipal Corporation Act of 1835, which forced city councils to be run on democratic lines, giving male rate-payers the vote. Now the city council was responsible for the police force and local courts, where before law and order had been dealt with by the militia. Crime was a big problem – it was calculated that the proportion of 'known bad characters' in the general population was one-third.

The council also had to take over health provision, poor relief, streets and sewers, and had to act as trustee for the municipal charities, which it was said had been robbed of £44,000 by the previous regime. Local parish councils were responsible for raising the

Detail from William Muller's oil painting *The Bristol Riots: the burning of the Bishop's Palace*, 1831. [Bristol Museums and Art Gallery]

poor rate, for highway maintenance and lighting – the central area and parts of Clifton by this stage had some gas lighting.

The council accounts were to be audited, so that there would be no more extravagant spending on drink, dinners and processions, as had been the case with the previous self-elected and corrupt regime. When Bristol Corporation was formed, there were enormous debts to be paid off, and huge sums in compensation were due to merchants and property owners who had lost everything in the Bristol Riots.

One important area where the council did not have sway was the city docks; the councillors were directors but did not have overall control and this was to have serious economic consequences. Another was in education, which was the concern of charities, religious bodies and private citizens.

The new city boundaries now took in Clifton, part of Westbury-on-Trym, part of Bedminster, St Pauls, St James, St Philip and St Jacob and these boundaries persisted throughout Victoria's reign. There were to be 16 wards electing 16 aldermen and 48 councillors; the aldermen had to serve six years, the councillors three and then stand for re-election. The mayor had to be elected by the councillors annually. Previously, the council members held office for life. According to the 1831 census, before these new boundaries the population was 110,000 and from then on the city was to expand considerably every decade, so that when the Queen died in 1901, the population of the city had trebled to 339,103.

To a modern time traveller, much of the 1837 city would be recognisable. The Georgian sections of the city were complete, Clifton was mostly developed, and many landmark buildings would be familiar: the Corn Exchange, the Old Council House, the Commercial Rooms, the Old Library in King Street, the Theatre Royal and the Coopers' Hall, the Bristol Institution (now the Masonic Lodge) at the bottom of Park Street, the

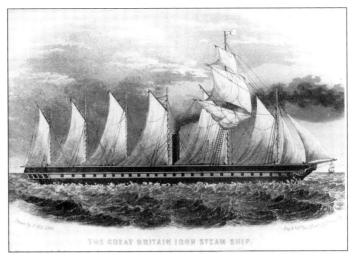

THE GREAT BRITAIN IRON STEAM SHIP.

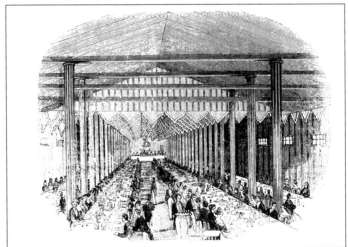

A banquet for 600 guests was held on board the *Great Britain* to mark the launching of the great ship in 1843.

Mansion House (now the Georgian House) in Great George Street, Red Lodge, Bristol Bridge, and the newly-built Custom House in Queen Square – the old one had been burned down in the Bristol Riots.

In Clifton, Royal York Crescent had been completed, Vyvyan Terrace and the Promenade has just been erected, and the foundations of the pro-Cathedral laid; plans were afoot to build the Victoria Rooms. Victoria Square was partly built.

The long battle to build the Clifton Suspension Bridge moved a stage further forward in 1837, for the Leigh Woods abutment foundation had been laid the previous year. A time capsule was placed underneath consisting of coins, a china plate with a picture of the proposed bridge on it, a copy of the Act of Parliament and a plaque describing the details of the work and its dimensions – presumably all still there. To ferry the Suspension Bridge workforce across the Avon Gorge, an iron bar had been placed between the two pier foundations, providing an exciting journey for those visitors brave

A bucolic Brandon Hill overlooking the city's smoke.

enough to try the crossing in a basket pulled by ropes.

What would not be recognisable was the open, stinking River Frome, filthy and disease-ridden, and the tangle of inner city slums, courts and alleys, the hundreds of dilapidated Tudor and Jacobean timbered buildings, and the ships in the city centre. There was no general public water supply, or sewers, and the filth and the smell would have been unbearable. Mortality rates in Bristol, one of the unhealthiest cities in the land, were appalling, with nearly half the children born dying before they reached their fifth year. Cholera and typhoid were endemic, as was TB.

To meet the high mortality rate, Arno's Vale Cemetery had been established in that year by Act of Parliament (on land originally destined for the Zoo) and the two lodges at the gates had been built. On the health front, Bristol General Hospital had been founded in 1832, and Bristol Medical School in 1833. Over 100 surgeons were listed in the 1837 street directory, along with six dentists and six manufacturing chemists.

Bristol was the third largest city in the country. In the eighteenth century, it had been the second port in the land, but by 1837 the trade with the West Indies, which comprised half of Bristol's overseas trade, was declining, partly because of the abolition of slavery but also because of competition, chiefly from Liverpool.

Local manufacturing and retailing for home consumption was becoming more important, the most successful being tobacco, cocoa, engineering and brewing. Some of these firms, albeit with new names and owners, are still trading: Wills and Frys, Avery's the wine merchant, Brooks the cleaners, Chilcott and Parsons the jewellery shops, the SPCK, and George's bookshop, now Blackwells, the law firms Latcham, Osborne,

A mid-century montage: Clifton Hill, The Victoria Rooms, Hotwells.

Announcement of the first Chartist meeting in Bristol.

Bevan and Burges Salmon, Ross the legal stationer, Roberts the market gardeners, Garaways the seed and plant merchants, Georges brewery, now Courage, Cowlins the builders, Dunscombe the optician, Gardiners, the iron merchants, and Clarks Wood, the timber merchant, were all trading in 1837.

There were rumblings of discontent among the working classes in 1837, and a branch of the Working Men's Association was formed after a public meeting held, alarmingly for the city fathers, in Queen Square, the very place where discontent had turned into riot a few years earlier. The handbills said the purpose of the meeting was 'to make a Declaration of our Political principles and to appeal to our fellow Citizens on the necessity of Union to carry those principles into effect. Working Men of Bristol! Arouse from your apathy, learn your rights, and how to maintain them!'

The speaker was Henry Vincent, a young printer who was to become the Chartists' spokesman for the West region, and he appealed to class solidarity, asking his audience: 'Was it meet that they who produced by their labour every luxury that the titled aristocracy and the moneymongers enjoyed, should be branded as ignorant slaves, and remain unrepresented in the Commons's House of Parliament?' The meeting passed resolutions in favour of a universal right to vote, with no property qualification, and a secret ballot.

As for education, according to *Matthews Directory*, in 1837 there were 40 ladies' boarding schools and 42 day schools, 18 boarding schools for young gentlemen, two preparatory schools for boys, and 11 endowed or charity schools, of which Bristol Grammar, Queen Elizabeth's Hospital, Colston's and Red Maids survive. Literacy rates were improving, if the listing of 54 booksellers in the city was any indication. There was only one public library, in King Street.

Also in existence in 1837 were two benevolent Sunday schools held daily, a British School, a Methodist Sunday School, St James's Sunday School, School for the Sons of Seamen, an Asylum for Poor Orphan Girls at Hooks Mills, a Baptist Church School, a Deaf and Blind Asylum, and one school each run by the Wesleyan Methodists, the Unitarians, the Roman Catholics, the British Irish, plus seven infant schools.

For leisure and entertainment, there were still horse races on Durdham Down in 1837, though this was the last year when major meetings were held from May through the summer. They were held in the area by Sea Walls, then called Wallis's Walls after the man who built them to prevent people falling into the Gorge, on a flat circular track, flanked by temporary grandstands, and the two-day events attracted entries from all over the country for the four-mile races. Prizes could be as much as 100 sovereigns, and the finest prize was the Bristol Cup, now in the possession of the Merchant Venturers.

Thousands of race-goers came by carriage or on horseback, and paraded in fashionable clothes, placed bets in the canvas booths and socialised, and the pickpockets had a fine haul. The scene is well captured in a painting by Rolinda Sharples. Organised sport was not common in 1837, though by then Clifton's Cricket Club was 18 years old.

The struggling Theatre Royal, newly-decorated by manager Sarah McCready 'in Raphaelite style with allegorical figures, landscapes and medallions of famous writers' put on not only plays but concerts, fancy dress balls, and even a circus.

The Zoological Gardens, admission fee one shilling, had recently opened, and by 1837 had 'a young tigress, a fine leopard, a camel, two sloth bears, a very fine antelope and many worthy specimens of the feathered tribe'. Appeals made to sea captains to bring back exotic creatures produced a fine young African male leopard, and a curious sheep with short hair spotted like a dog. An offer of a circus elephant was turned down through lack of funds but later that year, the Zoo bought its first elephant for £270. It died within two years.

1837 was the last year that the raucous St James's Fair took place. The fair had been going since the seventeenth century and in its heyday had attracted trade from all over Europe and even from Russia. (The closure was bad luck for James Ryan, a circus proprietor who that same year had opened a permanent arena near the Full Moon in Stokes Croft to attract the fair-goers.) The Council negotiated with St James's Church, who owned the land, and they agreed to abolish the Fair the following year. The ground was turned into a coal and hay market – hence the name of the street to this day.

Drink and drunkenness was a major pleasure and concern. The temperance and teetotal societies were fighting the results of the Beer Act of 1830, when duty was abolished; the Act allowed anyone to open a beerhouse 24 hours a day without control by the magistrates. The number of public houses per head of population was high and preventing the working classes from drinking too much was to become a middle-class hobby – 1837 was the year the Western Temperance League was formed, and Bristol Teetotal Society celebrated its first anniversary with 1,000 members.

Bristol was awash with drinking places in 1837, and some of them are still around: the Adam and Eve, the Spring Gardens, The Bear, the Bathurst Hotel (now the Louisiana), the Bunch of Grapes, the Bay Horse, the Clifton Tap, Four Stars, Full Moon, Hope and Anchor, The Plume of Feathers, the Ostrich, the Shakespeare Tavern, the Stag and

Hounds, the Three Horseshoes, the Ship and the White Hart all survive. And drink still causes problems.

The year 1837 was a watershed for Bristol and its social and economic future. How would the city fare in Victoria's age?

Snapshots of 1837

The death of King William IV, by Lavinia of Clifton
The kingly soul is free,
For the silver cord is rent in twain,
The weary throbs of a life of pain,
Defied captivity.
Felix Farley's Journal, June 1837

The accession of Queen Victoria
Much sympathy was felt for one called to the cares of sovereignty at so early an age. It must be added in the interests of truth that the attachment of the people to the monarchy had been rudely shaken by the experience of the previous quarter of a century, and the opinion expressed at about this time by Sir Robert Peel that the throne was visibly hastening to its fall, denoted the critical condition of the public mind.
Latimer's Annals of Bristol in the Nineteenth Century

The launch of Brunel's *Great Western* at Patterson's yard, July 22, 1837
This imposing ceremony took place on Wednesday and the weather being highly propitious, the scene was fine, if not the gayest and most interesting we ever witnessed. At an early hour all classes of citizens and thousands of persons from the surrounding country, in holiday dress, were seen wending their way to the place of attraction, and long before the launch was made, the several situations which commanded a view were densely thronged by a multitude to the amount of 50,000 at least. At 5 minutes past 10, the dog-shores having been struck away, the screw was applied and a general shout arose – 'She moves!'

During her progress off the slips, the most intense interest was visible on the countenances of the vast throng, and the beautiful and magnificent vessel had glided into her adopted element, which it did like a 'thing of life' and floated gracefully and steadily on the water. The multitudes in every direction rent the air with their acclamations.
Felix Farley's Journal

Brunel on the building of the GWR
If I ever go mad, I shall have the ghost of the railway walking before me, or rather standing in front of me, holding out its hand and when it steps forward, a little swarm

The Quay, St Augustine's Back and St Mary Redcliffe Church and Redcliffe Parade. Engravings from John Britton, 1829.

of devils in the shape of leaky pickle tanks, half-finished stations, sinking embankments, broken screws, missing guardplates, unfinished drawings and sketches will quietly and as a matter of course, lift up my ghost and put him off a little further than before.
Letter from Brunel to his friend Charles Saunders, December 1837

The foundation stone of the Great Western Cotton Factory was laid in Barton Hill
The introduction of this source of prosperity in Bristol had long engaged public attention but it was not until 1837 that active measures were taken to effect it by the association of

several of the leading inhabitants of the city with an eminent manufacturer of Manchester.
Chilcott's Guide

The new Zoological gardens

The Zoological collection is, we believe, at this time as extensive and valuable as most other similar establishments. The lake is universally considered to be the best specimen of 'ornamental water' in the vicinity; and together with the tastefully erected rock-work, that seems, as it were, to rise up from its bosom, present a picture of very unique and pleasing interest, and cannot fail to call forth the full admiration of the visitors.
Chilcott's Guide

Ryan's Stokes Croft Circus

This Superior Edifice is supported by 42 square columns and calculated to hold with a good view of the stage and circle, 2,000 spectators. The Boxes are all covered with cloth of soft texture, and the Pit is commodious and well-aired. The Gallery, large and peculiarly adapted for seeing, hearing and comfort, the Stage, built for the display of scenic illusions, processions over lofty bridges, combats, horse and foot, Spectacles, Melodrama, Comic Pantomimes and Grand Operatic Ballets.
The Bristol Mercury, 1837
(The domed roof of the building was a local landmark until it burned down in 1885)

St James's Fair, 1837

It had become a saturnalia. Foreign traders amounted to only a dozen and the tolls scarcely defrayed the cost of the stalls: the Fair lasted nine days and became the cause of a huge increase in crime, drunkenness and disorder, and the sideshows became a centre of corruption and demoralisation.
Latimer's Annals of Bristol

Bristol Madrigal Society is founded in 1837

They met at the Montague Inn, Kingsdown, with the aim of 'promoting Madrigal singing in this city'. The choir was to be men only, with boy trebles, and the singers sat around a large table. At their first meeting, the two trebles, six male altos, eight tenors and seven basses sang works by Wilbye, Weelkes, Gibbons, and Morley.

A Clifton Attraction

The Promenade, Clifton Hill, where there is an agreeable walking room, covered, floored and glazed, looking into a beautiful garden. The walk under cover is upwards of 350ft long; in some parts about 16 feet wide, in others 60–70 feet, with seven pairs of glass folding doors. It is well adapted for music, and any large assembly, as the voice is perfectly heard in the whole extent (if intended) without great exertion; it might also be used as a Bazaar or for any public purposes. It has a strikingly unique and pleasing effect. The garden, which it partly borders is laid out in gravel walks so as to be always dry.
Matthews Directory, 1837. Where could it have been?

Terms of Miss Dive's Seminary for Young Ladies

Broad instruction in the English language, Geography, History, Writing and Arithmetic, 26 gns. per annum, Extras Music, French and Drawing. Strict attention paid to morals and comforts of pupils.

Felix Farley's Bristol Journal, 1837

George Muller opens his third Orphan House in Wilson Street in 1837

This morning we received a parcel with clothes and some money for the Orphans from a sister at a distance. Among the donations in money was a little legacy, amounting to six shillings and sixpence halfpenny, from a dear boy who had died in the faith. This dear child had given to her on his last illness some coins. Shortly before he fell asleep he requested that this his little treasure might be sent to the Orphans. This precious little legacy is the first we ever had.

On December 17 he wrote:

This morning I saw the 32 Orphan girls, who are above seven years old, pass under my window to go to the chapel. When I saw these dear children in their clean dresses and their comfortable warm cloaks, and when I saw them walking orderly under the care of a sister, to the chapel, I felt grateful to God that I had been made the instrument of providing for them, seeing that they are all better off, both as regards temporal and spiritual things, than they were at the places from whence they were taken.

Muller's Journal

Crossing the Avon Gorge in a basket

On this fragile-looking thread a wicker car travels from side to side with visitors who are courageous enough to trust themselves to it, and this is quite as fearful as it looks.

Bristol Bridge looking towards High Street, engraving from John Britton, 1829.

We were adventurous enough ourselves once to go across, and the sensations we experienced are still vivid in our brain. A little wooden house is built on the edge of the cliff to keep the car in, and from this spot the adventure starts. To sit in the basket whilst the men in attendance are preparing to let go, and to look along the line, dropping in the centre as it does some 50 feet, is enough alone to make one slightly nervous but when the cry comes 'hold fast' and with the speed of light you rush down, as you fancy for the moment into eternity, the stoutest grip the sides of the wicker car with a convulsive strength and lift themselves as though the world was falling from beneath them.

As you get towards the middle of the passage, the speed decreases and after rising up for some little time on the other side, the car comes to a standstill; and now being halfway over, and the strange feeling in your stomach, which is the swallow-like rush down the wind has given you, having a little subsided, leisure is afforded to gaze about, and if you have the courage to look down, some idea of the height at which you hang suspended may be gained by the flights of rooks that, frightened by the passage of the car, whirl far beneath you, the sun shining like so much gold upon their backs. A rope attached to the basket pulls it up the ascending bar to the landing place on the opposite side. You give one shilling to perform this exciting journey.

The Land We Live In, A Pictorial and Literary Sketchbook, Part XII

Police regulations, 1837

The Principal object of the police establishment is the Prevention of Crime. To this end every effort is to be directed: the public security of persons and property and the preservation of public tranquillity and good order in the Borough will be better effected by the detention and punishment of offenders after they have succeeded in violating the laws. He (the Constable) must visit every part of his beat as often as possible, walking at the rate of two and a half miles in every hour, in order that any person requesting assistance may by remaining in one place for a short time, be able to meet with a constable.

Prison report on Bridewell Gaol, 1837

The inspectors were convinced that the present discipline of the gaol is defective in the highest degree. It is subversive of all moral principle, and in its effects must banish every reasonable hope of reclaiming the inmates of the gaol to a sense of their duty as members of a civil society. In proof of this, it is sufficient to state that persons committed for offences of the most trivial character and for the most atrocious crimes are constantly associating together. In the prison yard the same pernicious system exists … and to commit a fellow creature to the gaol in its present state is to consign him to almost irretrievable infamy and ruin, and to prepare society for inconceivable mischief.

Auction at the Commercial Rooms, August 1837

A valuable and commodious residence called Somerset House, between Upper and Lower Harley Place, in the immediate vicinity of the Zoo Gardens in the most attractive and desirable part of Clifton. It contains 4 principal apartments of good proportions; airy sleeping rooms; servants' rooms; a suitable arrangement of domestic offices; large rain-water cistern; spacious cellarage and stabling, coach house and walled garden in a good state of cultivation, commanding delightful views of Clifton, Durdham Downs, Leigh Woods, etc., and complete with all conveniences for a respectable family or well calculated for any Academical Establishment. The property is held under the Society of Merchant Venturers for a renewable term of 40 years and subject to an annual ground rent of 6 gns.

Felix Farley's Journal

Cornish broccoli comes to Bristol in 1837

Spring produce in Bristol suffered from repeated frosts, so new trade with Cornwall began. 'Mr Dupen, master of a steamer plying to and from Hayle, brought on one occasion about 50 Cornish broccoli which Bristolians eagerly purchased. About 15 dozen were brought in on his next trip and 60 dozen the following week.'

Latimer's Annals of Bristol

The last duel fought in Bristol

On the Downs, in January 1837, between a gentleman of the Hotwells and a foreigner residing in this neighbourhood. After an exchange of shots, the seconds succeeded in effecting an arrangement.

Latimer's Annals of Bristol

overleaf : One of Bristol's best known Victorian images: two workmen in Redland, 1850s.
[Bristol Record Office]

2 – Work: Virtute et Industria

THE STREET NAMES SAY IT ALL.

Anchor Road, Dock Gate Lane, Gas Ferry Road, Great Western Lane, Smoke Lane, Blackswarth Road, Brick Street, The Tanyard, Acraman's Road, Limekiln Lane, Foundry Lane, Boiling Wells Lane, Combfactory Lane, Rackhay, Pithay, Acid Road, Zinc Road. Bristol in 1837 was an industrial centre, and the industry was based right in the heart of the city.

Bristol had had its industrial revolution early, and by 1837 was recovering from the depression caused by the Napoleonic wars. It was still near the top of the league of provincial cities, though during Victoria's reign it was to drop to ninth place.

The centre of Bristol was a filthy, smoky, noisy, polluted district of factories, furnaces, smokestacks and sweatshops, of warrens of sixteenth- and seventeenth-century slum houses bordering on the stinking, sewage-filled River Frome which ran through the heart of the city. The mortality rate was one of the highest in the country.

Because Bristol had always had a mixed economy with a wide range of industries – pottery, sugar, glass, brass, soap, tobacco, coal, chocolate, cotton, printing, brewing, wine, bootmaking, pin-making, ironfounding, as well as the shipbuilding and dock trade – it fared better than the cities which relied on one group of industries, so that when there was a slump in one industry, the fall-out was restricted.

Bristol also had another great advantage – its association with Isambard Kingdom Brunel, who did wonders for Bristol's image as a forward-looking engineering city. With the Great Western Railway and the pioneering ships, the *Great Western* and *Great Britain*, and the Suspension Bridge, Bristol could have kept its place in the provincial league table. But a conservative council, and a docks policy which failed to realise Brunel's great ships were a threat as well as a blessing, delayed modernisation of the port until it was too late.

So prosperity depended mainly on manufacturing and here Bristol had another piece of luck, for the city was a seat of non-conformism, and many of the biggest industrialists were non-conformists: the Wills family, the Frys, the Sturges, the Robinsons ran their businesses in an enlightened way that produced good financial results – they saw caring for the physical and spiritual welfare of their employees as their religious duty. And it also helped that many of their employees were girls and women, which brought the wage-bill down. In fact wages in Bristol were generally lower than those in cities of comparable size.

Redcliffe from the tower of St Mary Redcliffe: houses and industry cheek-by-jowl.

Inspectors' reports on these factories were always approving: the staff were fed, educated and entertained, there were libraries, Sunday schools, outings, rest rooms, and to get a job in one of these firms was a triumph and a job for life. As an example of enlightened self-interest, the first Wills works outing was in 1851, when the 120 employees, who had each been given a sovereign to spend, went by GWR train and horse-bus to the Great Exhibition at Crystal Palace, where they saw the stands featuring tobacco production. It was the first time on a train for most of them, let alone the first visit to London.

Throughout the century these firms increased their profits, and dominated the national scene. By 1901, Wills was the largest producer of tobacco goods in the UK; while by the turn of the century Fry's, the first manufacturer of milk chocolate in Britain, was spending over £150,000 a year on advertising, and employing over 4,000 staff in eight new factories.

The major employers also influenced the development of the suburbs, for thousands of terraced houses were built in Southville, Bedminster, Barton Hill and Kingswood, to house local factory workers.

On the other side of the coin were the sweatshops, hundreds of them, crammed into houses and courts, where women and children worked from dawn to dusk on piece work, in dangerous insanitary conditions. Victorian prosperity also gave rise to the massive employment and exploitation of domestic servants, a topic dealt with in another chapter. And the biggest employers of all throughout the century were the boot and shoe manufacturers, who until late in the century relied on poorly paid out-workers and piece work; they employed 14 per cent of the labour force in 1841, and again 14 per cent in 1901.

Most working conditions were poor, and Government inspections went on throughout the century. An 1842 report by Dr Leonard Stewart on the employment of children and conditions at Bedminster collieries, found that 'boys were employed underground from the age of eight years and were used in opening and shutting doors to regulate the

Proctor's Cathay Chemical Works in the 1850s.

current of air. They worked 12 hours a day and received 4d. a day. Slightly older boys were employed at piece work as carriage boys to shove the coal along the level in carts or hudges. The low galleries were damp and cold and lit by candles. Boys wore a belt and harness to drag carts in the cramped tunnels. The manager, Moses Reynolds, said colliery boys drank and could not read or write though a few attended Sunday School.'

Parliamentary Commissioner Elijah Waring visiting in 1843 to inquire into trades and manufactures, found the Bristol Cut Nail Company in Wilder Street had many boys from nine years of age employed to attend the nail-cutting machines. 'The boys are chiefly sons of agricultural labourers living several miles from the city. They bring their meals with them, usually bread and butter: they rarely have meat. They are a rather unmanageable set and sometimes strike for more wages.'

He also visited the Pin Manufactory in Two Mile Hill, which employed 160 people including 110 women and children, while another 500 women and children were employed as outworkers. 'They work 6am–6pm, and in the factory a fine of 3d. is inflicted on any female who uses bad language or sings a profane song; they sing a good deal but are permitted only hymn tunes, of which there is a great variety.'

It was the eventual concern for health, after the damning public health report of 1845, and various Factory Acts that slowly changed working life for the lower classes. With slightly better working conditions, health improved, and working hours, though still long – 12 hours a day and a six-day week and no holidays other than Bank Holidays – were reduced. The needs of a newly wealthy middle class created employment in retail and manufacturing and there was a housing boom from the 1860s to the 1880s which provided thousands of jobs. The city docks, which had been taken over by the Corporation in 1846, were gradually modernised, with a new dock at Avonmouth in 1877, and at Portishead in 1879, even if it was too late to save the transatlantic trade

At the Victorian wash-tub.
[Bristol Record Office]

which had gone to Liverpool. Bristol's earlier periods of economic decline had been partly due to the reactionary docks policy.

The job opportunities in the city also attracted workers from rural areas, and the population had doubled to over 300,000 by the time of Victoria's death in 1901. The size of the city doubled too: entire new suburbs were born during her reign, at Bishopston and Horfield, Fishponds and St George, Ashley Down and St Andrews. Rows of Victorian terraces and villas, named Dunraven and Carisbrook and Waverley, still stand as testimony to Victorian prosperity, at least for the skilled masses.

Some industries such as glass, sugar, iron and coal had declined over the century, but the innovators thrived, notably the industries that were developed to serve existing trades – Mardons and Robinsons were set up to serve the print and packaging needs of firms such as Wills and Frys, both of which became national players. Fry's sales rose almost tenfold between 1836 and 1867 – the consumption of cocoa nationally doubled between 1841 and 1868, for it was sold as a health food. Eating chocolate, sticks and drops were introduced in 1850, and chocolate creams in 1855. Frys had only 193 employees in 1867, but by 1901, there were nearly 5,000. The company believed in the power of advertising and spent a then astronomical £2,000 on it in 1866.

Working-class confidence in its economic power was proved by the growth of trade unionism and by the series of strikes, notably in the boot and shoe sector and in the

Frog Lane Colliery, Coalpit Heath: miners in the transport cage. Coal was mined here until 1949. [from *City Pit* by Fred Moss]

docks. Most Bristol wages for men were lower than in other cities, and they faced greater competition from women workers, who traditionally were anti-union. Unionisation was gradual but by 1861 28 trade organisations and societies were established, and the Trades Council was set up in 1873.

The biggest period of union unrest was 1889–92, when iron workers and gas workers, dockers, stay makers, cotton operatives, brickmakers, hatters, sweet girls, brush makers, oil and colours men, coal carriers, scavengers, tramway workers, pipe-makers, hauliers and above all boot and shoe makers, all at some time went on strike for more pay and better working conditions. Many had bloody confrontations with the police and the militia, as happened when the dockers' strike procession tried to go over Bristol Bridge in 1892.

Chief-Superintendent James Cann reported: 'I heard a noise and saw a large concourse of people coming up the Welsh Back at a running pace. There was no semblance of a

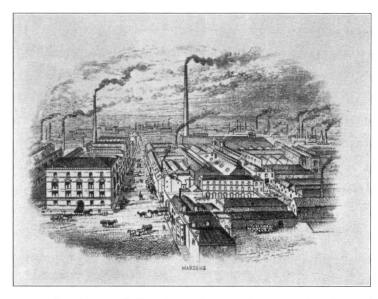

Broad Plain Soap and Candle Works c.1855.

procession, it was all disorder ... the crowd came on hooting and making a very great noise ... I judge there were not less than 500 people. They occupied the whole of the road and foot passengers ran to get out of their way. I and other police officers there held up our hands and shouted and endeavoured to stop them but they broke through the rank of police. I turned my head to the left to give an instruction and received a hearty blow to my chest which knocked me down.

'As I fell eight or a dozen fell on me. I was underneath a number of men. I struggled and extricated myself as quick as I could and I saw a constable lying on the ground by the side of me. During this time a large number of men which I estimate at 400 or 500 had gone over us and up through Bridge Street ... the demeanour of the men was very threatening, standing in front of the police with their fists clenched, saying "we will go through". The Dragoons were called in to end it.'

The major employers in the city believed in paternalism, not trade unionism, and discouraged their workforce from joining. William Sturge issued a warning in 1896, 'I confess I am greatly alarmed at the increasing power of the working classes whose leaders carry on a crusade against capital and endeavour to imbue their followers with socialistic views. The constant strikes, the illegal means used to compel men to join them against their will, the brutal attacks on non-union men, lead me to the conclusion that trade unionism, as carried out in this country, is a cruel and relentless tyranny, destructive of liberty and fatal to many of the industries affected by it, which will be driven away to other countries.'

The female workforce was slow to unionise, as Emma Paterson found when she started the first-ever trade union for women, the National Union of Working Women, in Bristol in 1874. She argued that girls went into service to escape low pay in factories, and so

Conrad Finzel's sugar refinery on the Counterslip by Bristol Bridge, the site later occupied by George's and Courage's breweries.

found another kind of slavery, and that all needed the protection of a union.

Working conditions were better in the burgeoning service sector, stimulated by the new wealth of the middle classes and the spread of literacy brought about by the Compulsory Education Act of 1876. Another sign of mass literacy was the growing print industry and the increase in the number of newspapers; in 1831 Bristol had four weekly papers, but by 1901, there were five daily papers, and seven weeklies.

More white collar jobs became available – young men and women who might before have been manual workers or servants now became clerical workers and shop assistants. Bristol today is almost a non-industrial city, with service industries as its main earner, a trend which began in the second half of the nineteenth century when banks, building societies and insurance companies began to colonise the business heart of the city, in Corn Street, Clare Street and Baldwin Street. The Stock Exchange opened in 1845 and the Commercial Rooms had been open since 1810. Law was a well-established profession and Bristol's Law Society had pre-dated the London one.

Between 1850 and 1870, nine building societies were established, and there was also a huge development of public services, transport, water, gas and electricity, post, telegraph and telephone, all of which improved the quality of life, and encouraged the growth of the suburbs. By 1895 these service workers were complaining that Income Tax took three and a third per cent of their earnings.

So by 1901, the future looked shipshape, industry was thriving, Bristol had sorted out its transport system, built its first motor car, an aeroplane industry was in the making and civic pride was high. There was even a plan to harness the power of the Avon tidal flow to generate electricity …

Snapshots of Work

Industrial Bristol

St Philips and Temple Meads, two districts which lie to the east of the city and either side of the river are almost entirely given up to manufactories and there is perhaps no place in England which contains such a variety of them in so small a place.

As we pass along, one moment a huge glasshouse cone attracts our notice, the fierce glow of the great fires which we see through the open door making black silhouettes of the busy workmen who stand before it. The next move brings us to the place where the din of hammers proclaims an iron factory; then again tis some distillery or pottery or alkali works. The locomotive factory of Messrs. Stothard and Slaughter, one of the most extensive in Great Britain, is situated in St Philips and a peep into their workshop shows us goodly rows of these gleaming monsters, in different states of progress, some but gigantic skeletons, others puffing with their first trial, and just ready to be launched on their arrowy course.

Unlike the pits about Birmingham and in the north, those in the immediate neighbour-hood of the city, especially the Ashton and Bristol collieries, are situated in the midst of the most rural and beautiful scenery; verdure extends to the very pit mouths and the tire-less arm of the mighty giant steam engine, lifting like a plaything enormous loads out of the bowels of the earth, continually meets the eye as we clear a clump of trees or the brow of some flowery hillside.
The Land We Live In, c.1842

The Horrors of Socialism

We have seen, in the rear of Broadmead, facing the Lower Arcade, a building about 80 feet long, 70 feet wide, which is now being lifted up as a Hall of Science. The

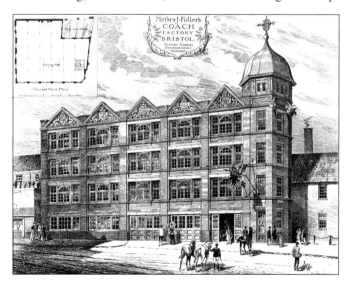

Design for Fuller's Coach Factory in St George's Road, behind the present Council House.
This fine building was demolished in 1970.

information that we can obtain concerning it is that it is taken by the Socialists and that it will probably be completed for the reception of votaries in three or four months... Where the funds come from to finish this expensive building is to us a mystery. When the Temple of Satan is opened for the sensual mysteries of the New Moral World it will be high time for parents, employers, and masters of families carefully to ascertain where all the young persons dependent on them spend their evenings.

Letter to Felix Farley's Journal, 1840

Matilda Bennett, aged 11, examined by an inspector, 1841

She is a painting girl at the Bristol Pottery. Has been so about two years, paints cups and saucers, comes from 6am to 6pm with a half an hour for breakfast and one hour for dinner. Sits at her work and is employed every day there is work. Is under Mr Marsh the foreman, who superintends but never beats her or treats her ill. Is paid as much as she earns and gets 4s. 6d. a week at most or sometimes 2s. 9d. Has her health very well and likes her work and her treatment.

Work at Fry's, Report of the Children's Employment Commission, 1866

The evident care bestowed in the comfort and welfare of the people employed here is such as befits the well-known family name which the firm bears, and makes it a pleasure to visit the place. The rooms are airy and cheerful, cleanliness prevails and the women and girls' work is well suited for them. The younger girls whom I spoke to had all been at school and said they could read.

There is a schoolroom and chapel into which every morning at a quarter to nine, after work had been going some time, the employees proceed looking bright and fresh, the men and the boys in canvas jackets, the girls in neat aprons. They sat down in an orderly way, each taking down a Bible from the shelves as they entered. The firm do everything they possibly can for the spiritual as well as the material well-being of their employees. A large room over the girls' factory is used as a reading room where every morning, the work people assemble to hear the scriptures read. The men are provided with a convenient room for their meals.

Report by Edward White, on Bristol working conditions, 1865

Bristol is a picturesque city, partly from its situation but chiefly from the age and character of the streets and buildings, many of which have the look of belonging to the middle ages. This however has the natural drawbacks in narrow streets and inconvenient buildings.

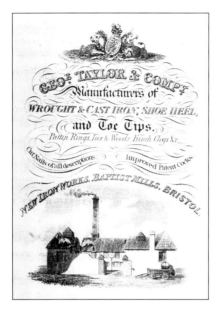

[White found that children were not made to work excessive hours but commented on the great want of proper privy accommodation.]

Thus at some place where at least 150 persons of both sexes are employed, there are only two privies, and in another there is only one for 100 or 150 men and boys. The places themselves are often choked up and in a filthy state.

Ben Tillett, trade unionist, remembers his birthplace

I was born in Easton, Bristol on September 11, 1860, in a tiny house in John Street, not many yards from East Coal Pit. It was a drab mean street and most of its inhabitants worked in the pit. The outlook was black, gaunt and smoky against the skyline. The buzz and musical clangour of the circular saw, swiftly cutting timber at pit prop length, driven by an engine with a deep-voiced exhaust, added to the industrial orchestra.

Ben Tillett's advice to Bristol strikers

You should attend church and chapel and pray that God might strike the employers with a human touch, that He might strike sympathy and nobleness into their hearts, to banish the selfishness, the blindness, and the greed that could not see the labourers' suffering.

The Sweet Girls go on strike

One of the girls at the factory was dismissed and this was followed by wholesale dismissal of 30 or 40 girls. The majority of the remainder are determined to work no longer until their comrades are re-instated. They complained of low wages, saying the majority of the girls, many of them grown women, received between three shillings and seven shillings a week and they had been refused the right of combination [joining a union]. So the girls would parade with sandwich boards and collecting boxes around the chapels on Sunday. In all 104 girls went on strike because, in consequence of re-arrangements in our departments we gave a girl notice to leave. We have had no difficulty in filling the places of the poor victims who have been induced to throw up their situations.

James Sanders, son of the owner of the confectionery works at 41 Redcliffe Street, 1892

Brightman Brothers, the boot manufacturers, ordered their workforce in 1883 to sign this declaration

I hereby declare that I am not a member of any trade unions or society having for its object interference between employers and employed, and undertake in the event of my joining any such society while I am employed by Brightman Brothers to give them immediate notice of my having done so with the understanding that it will subject me to immediate dismissal.

Deep Pit coal mine in the 1890s.

An experiment with electrical lighting, 1864

'The opening of the Suspension Bridge on December 8, 1864, was marked by a display by Mr Philips of Weston-super-Mare, who fitted arc lights at the top of each pier, two more in the centre of the bridge, two limelights at the base of each pier and four magnesium lamps in between,' the *Bristol Mercury* reported. 'At times the effect of the light was exceedingly brilliant, the rays being distinctly pencilled and elongated and all the outlines of the tracery of the bridge rendered clearly visible, while at others the light presented a dim appearance and caused great disappointment.'

The jubilee of John Breillat's gas experiments celebrated at Avon Street works, 1861

One of the extensive sheds where coal is stored, was cleared out and rendered presentable to the most fastidious eye. The roof was covered with evergreen and flags, and at either end, a pipe, bent in the shape of an arch was pierced in order that it might be illuminated in the evening. Some 200 sat down to tea. Among the venerable relics was one ancient pipe, wrought into a bust of His Majesty King George III, who in sombre and discoloured brass, was represented with a veritable crown upon his brow, from which shot up a number of rays, as the insignia of royalty was pierced with jets for that purpose. After tea the band began to play and tissue paper balloons were sent off with envelopes attached so those finding them could notify the senders of their resting place.
Bristol Daily Post

Concerned, Clifton writes about the gas supply

Sir, The Bristol people must be the most enduring of any on the face of the earth not to have complained about the wretched light that Bristol Gas Company are now giving us. What can be the cause? Has the weather anything to do with it or are the economies recently set on foot at the works to be held responsible for it? The lights in our houses are poor enough but they are no better at church, places of amusement or in the streets. The Gas Company charge quite enough for their product, and they ought in fairness to provide a better article.

A visit to Sheldon Bush shot tower, 1883

On reaching the summit of the tour we enter a moderately sized square apartment the walls of which are crusted over with a foul greenish deposit, a mixture of sulphur and arsenic, the sulphur emanating from the leading in fusion. In the centre of the room is a large melting pan, full of boiling metal, around being pigs of lead and a variety of tools required in the work. Beside the boiler is a pen trap door, over which one of the workmen presently places an iron stand. On top of this is securely fixed what is aptly termed a colander some 20 ins in length and about a foot wide, perforated at the bottom with innumerable small holes, according to the size of shot to be manufactured. On the surface of the molten lead and arsenic arises a thick scum … which acts as a kind of filter, allowing the fluid metal to pass slowly through the small holes at the bottom, in drops.

The Great Western Cotton Factory

An immense pile of building, for the purpose of cotton spinning and weaving has been erected on the margin of the Avon and the works are now in full operation having engines of 80 horsepower each and two of 20 each, constantly at work. The room at the front of the mills is the weaving room where about 700 persons chiefly young girls are employed making the yarn spun in the mill into cloth. The whole establishment is a perfect model of comfort and good arrangement and employs about 1,700 hands.
Chilcott's Guide, 1846

Working Girls at the Cotton Factory

Hundred upon hundreds of women and girls, with headgear consisting of shawls, mostly of a red and white plaid, but hanging over the shoulders, the quaint style of dress peculiar to their calling and formerly with wooden shoes, pattens on the pavement making the air merry with their peculiar sound. Such gigantic works as these, affording employment to so many females who might otherwise find it difficult to obtain work of a suitable character, cannot but be a very great direct benefit to the hands themselves while the indirect good resulting therefrom cannot be gauged.
Lesser Columbus, the alias of Leonard Cohen, 1893

Good behaviour

All male staff are instructed that all unnecessary familiarity with the opposite sex is to be avoided at all costs. Employees are warned that they are on no account to wander idly from department to department and those found singing, eating the firm's goods, entering beer shops outside working hours or acting with any impropriety are subject to the firm's and the family's strict censure.
Early working rules at Fry's

Wills dining hall menu

Meat and two veg, 4d., hot meat pie, 2d., bacon 2d. a slice, soup 1d., tea coffee or cocoa, 1d., aerated water, 1d., a bottle, plain cake 4d., per pound, slice of bread and butter, one halfpenny.

Backward Bristol

Most of the evils that Bristol is heir to are due to two causes. In the first place the people have a natural hereditary tendency to do as little as possible for themselves. The gospel of laisser-faire is more widely inculcated into the life of the Bristolian than of any other person. His father did without certain things and what is good enough for the father is good enough for the son. This succinctly explains the main cause for the reproach I must bring against the place – its backwardness. It is want of interest not want of heart, for the Bristolian is a capital fellow. He does not like to interfere.

Secondly, like city, like Corporation. It has done less for the city it misgoverns compared with any similar civic body. Most of the important towns in England own tramways, Bristol is the only large municipality in the country which allowed all these to be provided by private enterprise – when it is not public plunder.

But there is a new spirit arising in Bristol which knows not pusillanity. It has yet to attain the maturity and the vigorous activity of northern and midland enterprise but it is growing that way. The lethargy of Bristolians is not for all time. A more liberal tone will soon assert itself in its Council, in its magisterial appointments – and I do not even despair of a reform of its Aldermen. Bristol has all that makes for the extreme limits of commercial and social greatness.

Lesser Columbus, 1893

Too Old at Forty

We become unpopular with the people who employ labour. When we answer an advertisement they look dubiously at the tokens of honour appearing on our heads, the lines of experience crossing our faces, the mellowed way we walk into the office. And straightaway they shake their heads in the peculiarly decisive way we are getting used to. 'How old did you say? My dear fellow, you won't do. What we require is a young man … send your son along and we'll see.'

John Wall, trade unionist, 1901

overleaf : St George British School, 1895. [Reece Winstone Archive]

36

3 – Education: A little learning

IN 1837 MORE THAN A THIRD OF BRISTOLIANS would be unable to read this text.

One could argue that the greatest gift the Victorians gave us was mass literacy, for at the beginning of Victoria's reign, of the 20,000 Bristol children of elementary school age, only a quarter went to school. The rest grew up illiterate, as did their parents before them.

Education was optional and remained so until the 1870 Education Act, which created local education authorities and board schools. By 1876, elementary schooling was compulsory and by the end of the Queen's reign, school attendance in Bristol was up to 85 per cent, and there was free secondary education for those who qualified for it, at the newly built Merrywood, Fairfield and St George schools.

But back in 1837, education provision for the working class was piecemeal, patchy and voluntary, paid for by public subscription. Some 20 of these voluntary schools existed in 1837, and for those who could pay the fees, there were an astounding 82 private day and boarding schools for ladies, and 20 for young gentlemen. Bristol was slightly more fortunate than other cities, thanks to a remarkable number of endowed or charity schools – that year 15 of them are listed in the street directory, of which Colston's, QEH, Bristol Grammar School and Red Maids exist to this day.

These were schools with places to be awarded to the deserving poor, and designed to provide an education that would lead for boys to an apprenticeship in a trade and for girls, work as a servant. The regime was austere. There were also schools for orphans and for the sons and daughters of the impoverished professional classes, such as clergy or officers.

The inadequacies of education at the Bristol endowed charity schools were revealed by the 1864 Taunton Commission which has some scathing things to say about them. 'The educational aim in schools of this class is never high. The life lived in them is for the most part joyless and uninteresting. The children are dressed in a hideous costume, they are subject to restraints of a humiliating kind which are presumed to be appropriate at a charity school. The fact that all the scholars come from one class, and that a low one, causes the tone of thinking and the absence of stimulus or supervision from without renders the teachers satisfied with educational results of a most meagre kind.' It was, as the *Western Daily Press* commented, 'a lot to pay for teaching as little as possible, in order to produce servants for Clifton'.

This was the uninspiring routine at Red Maids: Girls rose at 6.30am, attended prayers at 7.30 and then went to breakfast. Morning school began at 9.15 with dictation, spelling and parsing, followed by geography, history from 10.15 to 10.45. Then until 11.45 there was singing, drill or play, and reading or walking occupied the time until dinner at 12.30. The girls played in the garden until afternoon lessons began at 2pm, with domestic economy until 3pm then needlework and singing until 5pm.

For the rest of the working class there was a scattering of schools run by church or chapel, and called British Schools if they were non-conformist, and National schools if they were Church of England. Here pupils had to pay twopence a week, a significant sum when to keep a large family, a father's earnings might be a few shillings a week.

School also had to compete with paid work for children, in factories or in home industries, so for the majority the only brush with the three Rs was at Sunday schools, some of which were open every day of the week. It was estimated that by 1851, nationally two million children were enrolled in Sunday schools. For the destitute children, there might be a place in a ragged school such as the one run in Lewin's Mead. It was not until 1867 that employment of children under seven was prohibited and this age limit was raised to 10 in 1873; the minimum age for working in a factory was raised to 11 in 1893.

For the next layer of society there were dozens of dame schools and academies, run by unqualified teachers offering whatever subjects they could scrape together. These attracted the aspiring lower-middle classes desperate to ensure that their sons and daughters grew up to be gentlemen and ladies. Some were day schools, some boarding, and the main purpose was not education but the acquisition of social skills, etiquette, the ability to draw and dance, and speak a little French. For girls the aim was to make them marriageable, for boys, to be fit to join their father's businesses. There were no inspections, no standard curriculum and no examinations.

There was one shining exception. One of the oldest girls' boarding schools in the country, Badminton School, was founded in Clifton in 1858 by Mrs. William Badock. The prospectus offered: 'French (which is made the medium of conversation) with a sound English education comprising Writing, Arithmetic, Grammar, Composition, Elocution, Biblical Knowledge, Geography, Ancient and Modern History, Natural Philosophy, Botany, Astronomy, Callisthenics, Deportment, Plain and Fancy Needlework.'

The annual fees were fifty guineas for boarders and twelve guineas for day pupils. The services of a laundress were available for three guineas, a seat in church for one guinea and each girl had to bring a silver fork and spoon. When Mrs Badock moved to Badminton House in Clifton, in 1868, she had a gymnasium built, one of the first in the country, and when she retired in 1893 there were 55 pupils.

The academies flourished throughout the century, with a few of them developing into respectable academic schools, but most only attracted a handful of pupils each, and closed or changed hands regularly. In Clifton alone there were 26 academies for girls listed in 1888. As Clifton educationist Catherine Winkworth remarked: 'Apart from the famous schools, secondary education is carried out in a large number of private schools

Clifton College: John Percival and staff in 1865. [Clifton College Archives]

for boys and girls. The healthiness and beauty of Clifton has rendered it a very favourite situation for ladies' schools and the number of them is very large; some are day schools, but there is no public day school for girls in this city.'

The wealthier middle classes and the local gentry would hire a governess for the girls and a tutor for the boys, and thanks to the new railway network could send the latter away at 13 to public school, at Marlborough or Cheltenham, since Bristol to its chagrin could not offer this type of education.

This was to be remedied in 1862 when Clifton College opened. It was offering something new, as the prospectus reveals. The purpose was 'of providing for the Sons of Gentlemen a thoroughly good and liberal Education at a moderate cost': Fees in 1862 were £25 a year for day boys, and £90 for boarders.

The syllabus offered pupils in the Lower School 'a sound elementary knowledge of Latin, Greek, English and Arithmetic. The Upper School will branch into two departments, of which the Classical will have special reference to the Universities, and will comprise all the subjects usually taught at a Public School, including French, German and Mathematics; in the second or Mathematical Department, the amount of Classical work will be diminished, while greater prominence will be given to Mathematics, Modern Language, English Literature, History and Composition.' Also in the curriculum was something unheard of: games.

There was also to be a laboratory, an art room, a library, all luxuries not offered by the academies, and it was promised that the proportion of masters to boys would be 'unusually large', a master to every 14 boys.

What Bristol parents liked about Clifton College was the muscular Christianity and the

Clifton College:
the school's fire
brigade, 1883.

high moral tone, as well as the emphasis on academic subjects, and the opening sermon, preached to 60 boys by the 25 year-old headmaster, John Percival, set out the College credo: Come here 'if you desire to belong to a place where all that is base and unworthy is hated and despised, a place where truth and uprightness and purity and all Christian virtues are held in honour. There is not a single boy who now hears me, down to the very youngest but may do something to win a worthy noble Christian character for this his place of education, if only he will do his best. And remember all of you that if any one among you do evil, that evil will not only defile his own heart, but will leave its stain on this unstained spot.'

The arrival of the College and its liberal staff led to two important educational developments: the setting up of an equally academic education for girls, with new establishments such as Clifton and Redland High Schools, and further education for women, and a university college, open to women as well as men, for the city. Clifton College raised standards, and made parents expect more from whatever school they chose. High

Colston's school band in 1894. [*Mr Colston's Hospital*, Society of Merchant Venturers]

schools however were considered in some quarters to be producers of bad-mannered blue-stockings who would never marry. They exposed girls to moral danger, since they had to travel on public transport; it made them rough and boyish, and some wore no gloves in the street.

The new high schools soon discovered how poor education for girls had been at the 'academies'. The headmistress of Redland High School commented: 'Many of the girls who come to us have been allowed to grow up to 13, 14, or even 15 years of age without ever having done any difficult or serious work.'

Meanwhile state education, an idea current even in the 1840s, was delayed again and again by councillors terrified of alienating the city rate-payers. It was also thought that educating the working classes might give them ideas above their station, and there was 'wordy warfare' over the denomination of the board schools – should they be undenominational, secular or Church of England?

But the arguments ended when responsibility for education was forced on local authorities by the 1870 Act, which required the setting up of Boards of Governors for each of four city districts, and for building and maintaining board schools and paying their staff, and 27,554 places had to be found. School attendance was made compulsory in 1876; at first parents paid but in 1891 education to the age of 12 was made free for every child.

Colston's schoolboy
in 1885.
[Mr Colston's Hospital,
Society of Merchant
Venturers]

When in 1875 Bristol was host to the national conference of the British Association, the handbook listed the breakdown of educational establishments in the city; there were 12 endowed schools, Muller's Orphanage school, 10 board schools, 21 ragged, industrial and reform schools, and 113 schools under inspection.

The new set-up had some strangely familiar aspects: a national curriculum, regular inspections, frequent tests to see if pupils had reached set targets for each 'standard' or class, a target for attendance, and for the staff, payment by results. Truancy officers roamed the Bristol streets and parents could be fined for keeping children home; in 1871, attendance officers – feared figures – made 51,534 home visits and issued 250 summonses for non-attendance, and a truancy school was set up. But it took time to get truancy rates down: in 1873 there was 70.7 per cent attendance, and by 1901, there were still 15 per cent who truanted.

These were the rules for the Bristol elementary board schools in 1871:

    Mixed classes with women teachers up to the age of seven.

    Segregated classes for children over seven.

    The Bible to be read to pupils but non-denominational teaching.

    A broad curriculum.

    Headmasters to be responsible for corporal punishment, which could not be administered by pupil teachers.

    Leaving age 13 but some exemptions 10–13.

    Fees 3d. a week up to third standard, 4d. above. Remission of fees for those unable to pay.

Corporal punishment was the norm. This was the Discipline Code for Bristol Board schools in 1884:

    Caning should be by the Headmaster on the back of the hand in front of the class.

    Boxing of the ears and cuffing by hand is not permitted.

    Infants should not be caned and girls only in extreme cases.

In the 1890s, if corporal punishment was needed for pupils who were taught privately at home or at an academy, parents could hire the services of a professional disciplinarian, Mrs Eliza Walters of Oakfield Road, Clifton. She advertised in *The Times*: 'Intractable girls trained and educated, advice by letter 5s.' This widow of a headmaster told a *Times* reporter how she strapped girls down on a table and administered strokes of the birch 'to the orthodox surface'. 'I measure my distance and proceed to strike slowly but firmly. By moving gently forward each stroke is differently placed and six strokes may be sufficient if well given with full force.' She charged half a guinea a treatment and had a full engagement book.

Another Victorian innovation was teacher training – the College of St Matthias at Fishponds was set up in 1853. Until 1846, when the first training colleges were established, voluntary schools used the monitor system, with the eldest becoming, if they wished, pupil teachers, who trained on the job. Properly trained teachers were sorely needed. The first Principal of St Matthias wrote: 'I took up my abode in the institution in August 1853. The matron arrived the following day. On September 10 we opened the training school with six students … and in the first decade 270 women trained for two years at a practising school for infants and girls.'

But there were rebellions against the conformist treadmill system of Victorian education. School strikes took place in the city in 1889, as part of a national campaign by pupils in sixty towns. Pupils paraded in the streets demanding shorter school terms and school hours and the abolition of corporal punishment and homework. The main grievance was homework and excessive use of the cane. The *Western Daily Press*, reporting the end of the strike, on October 5, said 'when the very children rise against authority, society is in a bad state'.

Thus education in Victorian Bristol gradually moved towards one academic standard for all, rather than an education tailored to class, and the great prize at the end of the century was mass literacy and numeracy. By 1901, seven out of ten Bristolians could sign their names, instead of putting a cross.

Snapshots of education

Rules for the Dings British School, 1842

Parents shall send their children to school clean in person, wearing no ornaments, and having their hair plainly and neatly arranged. Each child will be required to wear a pinafore and belt, which may be procured at the school … It is hoped that the day is coming when education will be universally regarded as the birthright of man and when to withhold intellectual and moral culture from minds created and placed within our reach shall be esteemed an injustice to society and a sin against God.

Mary Carpenter's ragged school

It was a wonderful spectacle to see Mary Carpenter sitting patiently before the large school gallery in St James's Back, teaching singing and praying with the wild street boys, in spite of endless interruptions caused by such proceedings as shooting marbles at any object behind her, whistling, stamping, fighting, shrieking out Amen in the middle of the prayer and sometimes rising en masse and tearing like a troop of bisons in hobnailed shoes down from the gallery, around the great schoolroom and into the street. These irrepressible outbreaks she bore with infinite good humour.
Frances Cobbe, in The Modern Review

Opening of the Ragged School, Lewin's Mead, 1846, recalled by the master in charge

That afternoon I shall never forget. Only thirteen or fourteen boys present; some swearing, some fighting, some crying. One boy stuck another boy's head through the window. I tried to offer up a short prayer, but found it was impossible. The boys, instead of kneeling, began to tumble over one another and to sing 'Jim Crow'.

Entries from the Hotwells Boys School logbook

September 21, 1863

Samuel Tomkins commenced his duties as master this morning. At nine o'clock six boys were present. During the day the boys were extremely disorderly, some fighting, pushing each other about, one boy being knocked down, injuring his face. Monitors shirking the children in their classes, and the older ones answering the master and exceedingly impertinent, apparently caring for nobody and nothing.

An inspection at Hotwells, 1879

I am sorry to have to speak once more and very strongly about the discipline. The pupil teachers have little control and Mr Hopton's oversight does not seem to be effective

Pupil Teachers' Centre, Broad Weir in 1899. The centre had first opened 10 years earlier in Castle Street.
[Samuel Loxton drawing, *Bristol: as it is and as it was*]

beyond the class he is teaching [more than one class shared a room] and his unfortunate noisy style is not calculated to secure quietness and order.

In the margin, the Headmaster has written 'What a hope!'

A report on Christ Church School Clifton, 1887

The well-disciplined and organised boys, whose singing deserves special praise, the orderly and well-behaved girls whose handwriting is far from satisfactory and spelling poor, though whose needlework had decidedly improved, the bright and cheerful infants who have been carefully and diligently taught. [This still surviving school was founded in 1852 in what is now Clifton library, and was paid for by public subscription.]

Aims of the Bristol Asylum for Poor Orphans at Hook Mills, a charity school

To rescue destitute children of this description from the contaminating examples of Idleness and Vice, to instil in their tender minds the principles of Religion and Morality and to inure them to habits of industry and cheerful obedience, by instructing and employing them in every kind of Householder work, which may qualify them for acceptable servants in Respectable Families.

Emma Williams of Highbury Chapel reports on the ragged school in Leadhouse Lane, St Philips, in 1870

Four cottages were rented for a Sunday school for the benefit of those children whose clothes were so worn and ragged that they could not attend any other school. Within a year the school had 140 children. 'They were dirty, ragged and rude. Their clothes, such as they were, had previously belonged to their parents or older brothers and sisters; they were tied with string and probably never taken off.'

Miss Williams noted the intolerable odour and the awful language, and teaching was an ordeal. On one occasion a boy tried to flood the class by leaning on a tap. The boys made a game of everything the teacher said and when there was a Sunday School outing to Weston-super-Mare there were terrible problems keeping them from getting unruly on the train, and with chasing the older ones out of public houses.

St Augustine's School logbook, 1885

Alexander Armstrong has been absent since Monday. I have several times asked his brother where he is, and he today told me that he has gone to Newport with his father for a short while and will come to school when he returned. Scarce believing this I have enquired about, and find a score of them have seen Alexander about the streets today and other days, helping another with a donkey and cart to sell coals.

Rules of Red Maids School, 1844

No parental visits allowed, girls may go home every fourth Monday; girls over 12 to do most of the housework and apart from that girls might not go into any part of the house except the school rooms and the playground. There will be fines for breakages and girls may have clean laundry once a week.

From *A Book of Bristol Sonnets* by Canon H Rawnsley, 1877

Red Maids School

Those hands unto the heart for help did send,

Who limned these red-skirt maidens, where they sit,

Weaving their humble futures as they knit,

Making a happy present as they mend!

Code at Queen Elizabeth Hospital, 1848–1888

Boys to be instructed for their future destination of apprentices to trades, clerks etc. In the schoolroom, at meals, and upon occasions on which the boys are assembled together or in gangs for the performance of any duty, they shall be silent and orderly.

Boys to wear uniform dress at home as well as in school.

Parents are not to visit except on Saturdays, 2–4pm (2–6pm in summer) and then only at the entrance lodge, except in sickness. [This rule was abolished in 1857.]

All masters to attend boys to church on Sunday and afterwards to instruct them in catechism and scripture.

Parents are not to supply boys with fruit etc., either at visits or on the way to church on Sunday.

Assistant masters to inspect boys at night after prayers, to see if their faces and hands are washed.

Memories of life at QEH in the 1870s

On Sundays we rose at 7.30am, went to St George's Church for Matins, attended the service taken by the Head in the Dining Hall after dinner, and read books from the special Sunday library from 7–8pm, books with improving moral lessons such as *Eric* or *Little by Little*. Sunday dinner was always boiled beef and beetroot. All the boys took their share in chores, cleaned their own shoes, made their beds, swept and cleaned their rooms and cleaned the wcs. Weekly baths (at Jacob's Wells) were held on Friday evenings. We were boiled, thirty at a time in the small swimming bath and dried ourselves in bath towels made of sheeting, so that it was quite impossible to dry one's skin thoroughly.

Morale at Colston's Boys, 1876

Five boys were suspended and later expelled for gross insubordination and dishonesty after a series of petty larcenies in the masters' dining room. They had apparently raided supplies of bread, butter and sugar during the night, on a number of occasions, opened two staff locks with a false key, and regaled themselves with biscuits, cocoa and methylated spirit under the supposition that it was gin. Furthermore their carousels were also enhanced by the smoking of cigars and cigarettes, the latter stolen by a young new boy from his mother's shop, after he had been induced to do so. No sooner had the headmaster obtained a clue which directed suspicion towards the five boys, than the two ringleaders absconded in the hope of escaping abroad by ship from Cardiff. Several other boys subscribed money towards the elopement of the two ringleaders, an example of the low moral tone of the school.

A harsh regime at Bristol Grammar School, 1868

A boy took a book from another's desk and sold it at a second-hand bookshop. He was expelled and others suffered the same fate for truancy, disobedience and falsehood, for 'persistency in filthy conversation and for passing spurious coin'.

Three respectable lads, scholars at the Bristol Grammar School, were charged with maliciously damaging public gas lamps, the property of Bristol Gas and Light Company. They had used catapults, not only against the gas lamps, but also against a cab and a gentleman on a horse. They were each fined £1 and costs and the magistrates told them they could have been given two months' imprisonment with hard labour.

Times and Mirror

Evidence taken in Bristol by the 1864 Taunton Commission inquiry into education

Mothers, one headmistress told the inspector, were acutely sensitive to anything which might have an adverse effect on their daughters' social standing. If any girl begins to get interested in the schoolwork and is seen in the evening busy over her theme, her mother comes to me and says: 'Now, Miss – you must not make Augusta a blue.' If I report that another does not try to improve herself in arithmetic, the mother says: 'Well you know I am anxious of course about her music, but it really doesn't matter about her arithmetic, does it? Her husband will be able to do all her accounts, you know.'

A governess in the 1860s

I fear she had a hard time with us, sometimes she was almost reduced to tears, 'Look,' said her tormentor, to the interested company of children sitting around the table, 'look at her, she's blubbing.' Miss W's accomplishments I suspect were not very great, but she could teach what she knew. She taught me all the arithmetic I ever learned. She took her troubles with her obstreperous pupils very good-humouredly. I often took her part for I was always sorry for our teachers and I remember hiding with her in the roomy closet of the large room in which we four girls slept.

Elizabeth Sturge, Reminiscences Of My Life

John Percival, first headmaster of Clifton College, preaches a sermon on Manliness

In this atmosphere you are expected to imbibe a love for manly tastes and pursuits, something of an active, enduring perservering spirit, something of a true contempt for effeminacy and indulgence and torpid do-nothing idleness. The more sickly and morbid elements of character are purged out of men by the discipline of a life such as yours.

Some Helps In School Life

A Clifton College master recalls the early years

The boys of those days had no notion of games or the respect due to them. You will hardly believe that we used to have to persuade the boys in those days, if it were at all wet in the afternoon, to take their coats off and play football, or go runs.

Clifton High School

Principles laid down by the first Headmistress, Mary A. Woods:

That the school should be non-class, ie open to all girls of good character, without social discrimination.

Clifton College juniors, 1893.

That it should be consistently non-denominational and that it should accord to the teaching staff the same religious freedom.

That it should be non-competitive, admitting neither prizes, marks nor place-taking but as far as possible making the interest of each the interest of all.

She later wrote: 'Readers acquainted with Clifton will readily understand the sort of criticism we encountered, criticism from parents who objected to what they called the 'mixture' ie. of classes, from heads of private schools who thought their interests endangered, or perhaps from a doting mother who demanded concessions to the educational style.'

Elizabeth Sturge on Lectures for Ladies, 1868

There were a large number of young women who could never hope to become students at Oxford or Cambridge – for their benefit a system of local lectures to ladies was established. We were fortunate in having in Clifton a circle of enlightened men and women by whom the idea was warmly taken up … Of course such a method of study was very unsystematic, one jumped from one subject to another, but the mental stimulus was of lasting value.

We read diligently and every week handed in papers signed by a number or pseudonym – such was the dread at that time of having your name known in such a connection. There was great excitement when the lists were read out – some, who had not attained the position they hoped for were even known to weep!

Reminiscences Of My Life

The Rev. Francis Kilvert visits Janet Vaughan at the Clergy Daughters' School, Great George Street, 1874

I did not know at first where to find the girls but the sound of two or three pianos guided me to the top of the street where stood a large old-fashioned red brick house in a pretty garden … Then girls came out with their books and work and soon all the shady nooks were full of light dresses and bright pretty faces and pleasant voices … upon some of the trees girls had carved their initials and upon the bark of a young beech whose bark was black with Bristol smuts I carved JV and reluctantly at her earnest request my own RFK above.

School uniform for Clergy Daughters' School [later St Brandon's] was 'an umbrella, comb and brushes, gloves, four day shifts, three night shifts, two pockets [aprons], two pairs of shoes, and thick boots or clogs, one coloured dressing gown, four brown Holland pinafores, work bag and sewing implements, two pairs of stays, two flannel petticoats, three white upper petticoats, one stiff petticoat, six handkerchiefs, six pairs of white cotton stockings, a Bible and a prayer book.'

Redland High School fourth-formers go to Paris, 1890

There was a slight fuss at Bristol Station on account of a misunderstanding about the Saloon Carriage that was to convey us to Paddington and in the confusion one of our number got left behind. The sea passage was not a pleasant one to some of our party and

Bristol Museum and Library, Queen's Road, 1867.
The ground floor is now Brown's Restaurant.

Dieppe did not impress me very favourably. At Dieppe we took a train to Paris, and our train collided with another one and the boiler burst, but after sundry stoppages and much exercising of patience, we arrived.

Former pupil Christopher Robinson remembers poverty at Baptist Mills National School in the 1890s

Every morning when we filed into school, we were asked the question 'Have you had any breakfast, son?' If the reply was 'No, sir', the boy was directed to a side classroom where he was given as much bread and treacle as he could eat and a good cup of tea. These free breakfasts were paid for by the schoolmaster and his teaching staff, with such help as they could get from friends and tradespeople. We were given cast-offs from Clifton or Redland, Eton jackets and morning suits, I think the sight that capped the lot was of the kids and their hats. Even in winter you would see nippers wearing straw boaters, and college caps were common. I think the limit was reached when one pupil sneaked round the corner of the school yard, wearing a mortar-board.

Scandal at Colston's Girls School, 1898

Headmistress Miss Smith suspended 17 girls from the school for having copied and circulated an immoral paper. The governors approved the action and expelled three; 14 girls were suspended until January and two exhibitions terminated. The whole school was sent home a day early and prize-giving postponed.

The first year at the College of St Matthias, Fishponds, 1853

The food was good, but there were no heating appliances and the winter of 1854 was bitterly cold. The students washed overnight as there was no water in the morning. Our dormitory cubicles had curtains instead of doors and on windy nights the students pinned the curtains to the partitions. The ground floor rooms were lighted with oil and the dormitories with candles – a candle in a tin candlestick was fixed at each alternate partition and when the governess, at 10 o'clock said, 'lights out' alternate students stood on their beds and blew out the lights. A fine of 2s. 6d. was imposed on any student found in the kitchen to warm themselves by the fire.

Early days at University College

Between 1876 and 1909 (when the University got its Charter) students attended University College for a variety of motives which varied from the trivial to the earnest. In the early days, there were numerous young ladies from Clifton, for example (some previously educated by a governess), who used the College as a type of finishing school. Young men too, who had perhaps entered a family business, came in for as little as a term to establish a minimal grasp of scientific principle, or to improve a chosen subject. Married women were not unknown and one left it on record that her classes were an excellent source of after-dinner conversation.

J Sherborne, University and Community, 1976

University College lectures

Electric lighting would be great improvement on gas and one hopes that lecture rooms are lit with it, to preserve us from the somnolence which comes over us on all such occasions and seriously debars us from enjoying them or gleaning instruction.

Helen Sturge letter, 1878

Dr Doudney's Soup Kitchen in Wlliam Street, Bedminster in the 1870s. The doctor is on the left.
[Reece Winstone Archive]

4 – The Underclass: The undeserving poor

ONE OF THE LEAST ATTRACTIVE ASPECTS of Victorian Bristol was its harsh attitude to the poor, and its use of charity for social engineering.

Bristol had been famous since medieval times for its myriad charities, yet Victorian Bristol was also a place notorious for its slums and the abject poverty of a large number of its citizens. The population had grown so much that the ancient charities could no longer cope with their needs.

An underclass had been created by a lethal mixture of poverty, ill health, unemployment and appalling housing. This led to vice, crime, drunkenness and violence, which in 1837, only six years after the Bristol Riots, produced in the rest of the citizens a constant fear of riot and disorder, and a desire for draconian measures to keep the underclass down. It was reported that year that Queen Square (parts of which were still in ruins) was attracting 'the scum of society. Gangs of boys and men are allowed to dig up the grass plots, play at pitch and toss, climb the trees for the birds' nests, hurling stones and using the most filthy language and gestures with impunity.'

The nature of the city itself created slums: the better-off had moved upwards to Clifton and Cotham and Redland, leaving behind the dilapidated Tudor and Jacobean buildings and the Georgian artisan terraces, which became teeming and dangerous tenements. The pressure on this inadequate housing grew with an influx of the rural poor seeking work in the factories of the industrial revolution.

Dozens of families would be crammed into courts, which were infills between buildings, narrow dark alleys with houses built either side, with a family to a room, and outside a standpipe and one shared privy. Disease spread like wildfire, crime was rife, and the unemployed, facing starvation, sent their children out begging in the streets. When Commissioner Sir Henry De La Beche came to Bristol during the 1840 enquiry into public health, he found conditions in one Bristol slum so disgusting that he had to go into an alley and vomit. The report found Bristol the third most unhealthy city in England. In 1844 a survey of 2,500 families in Bristol found that 46 per cent of them lived in one room.

Hotwells, St Philips, Redcliffe and Bedminster all had networks of these courts, often one leading to another through a tunnel, hidden behind the main streets, and unseen by the middle classes. At one time there were said to be 600 courts, most later swept away not by social conscience but by road-widening schemes and the Blitz; only a few examples are left, like Hanover Court by the side of the Hippodrome, and passages off Dean Lane and behind East Street, Bedminster.

Then there were the doss-houses where the 'penny hangers' slept leaning over a rope; these lodgings in the poorest slums of the city were known as flash houses or netherskens, and were homes for thieves, vagabonds and prostitutes. An attempt to control them came with the Common Lodging House Act of 1851, and the Inspector for Bristol managed to get 60 of them closed.

The Corporation did not see it as its role to build homes to rehouse the poor, or pay for repairs of substandard housing, or subsidise rents, until it was forced to by the 1890 Housing of the Working Classes Act. Between 1890 and 1900, only 300 homes out of thousands were then declared unfit for human habitation and condemned.

The Fabian Society published a statistical survey of Bristol in 1891, claiming that the city's record on housing was far worse than 27 other large towns in the country. They reckoned that 10,000 families needed to be rehoused.

'Thousands of Bristol families are huddled together in 600 courts and the very large number of houses without backlet [rear exit] are mostly unfit for human habitation, with an average of four persons per room. Notwithstanding these facts, no action has been taken by the Town Council under the Artisans' Dwellings Act to provide decent accommodation for the poorest citizens. At least a thousand of Bristol's citizens have no better home than the common lodging houses.'

The Fabians concluded that Bristol was also deficient in its provision and control of the education system, that there was no collective provision for the sick, and that the city and its council were not interested in 'municipal socialism'.

Yet improving housing worked, as Susannah Winkworth proved with her Industrial Dwellings built in 1874 in Jacobs Wells Road. She raised the money to build these new flats, lit by gas, with proper sanitation, running water and balconies, and the improvement in the morale and health of those who were lucky to get homes there was immediate.

Yet alongside this distrust and fear of the poor was the other great feature of the Victorian age, a do-gooding impulse, and a belief in progress and self-improvement. Charities abounded; apart from Bristol Municipal Charities, which in 1836 took over from the Corporation administration of the famous old charities of the city, there were hundreds of charitable organisations, run by churches and chapels, by titled ladies, by middle-class matrons, concerned spinsters, or local dignitaries.

This set-up was possible because those women who had become middle-class could no longer have paid occupations; the wives and daughters now had servants and thus a huge amount of leisure time to fill. Charity work filled it; they could spend all year making fancy goods for the grand annual bazaar, they could collect clothing and blankets for their local church, give small sums to various charities, all without actually having to see the (deserving) poor who benefited. It was a piecemeal, unco-ordinated affair, where money did not always reach the people who needed it most. Only a tiny percentage of

Steep Street in the 1860s.

the charitable citizens actually worked alongside the poor in missions and soup kitchens.

The major charities were concerned with funding schools, hospitals, asylums and almshouses; the smaller charities with providing domestic instruction, food, clothing, blankets, medical treatment, and small sums of cash, but such help went only to the deserving and respectable poor. A modern equivalent would be to restrict welfare benefits to Christian, legitimate, non-smoking, teetotal, married claimants.

Charities often worked on a subscription system: the donor would be given so many notes, according to the size of the subscription, usually four notes per guinea gifted, and these notes would be handed out to the poor who made the best case for help: the Dispensary in Dowry Square worked on this principle. Often sick people would have to go from subscriber to subscriber, pleading for a note for free treatment. This was said to 'promote a spirit of independence among the labouring classes'.

They were also intent on reforming those who had turned to a life of vice and crime, funding institutions like the Bristol Female Penitentiary, which received 'those unhappy females who departed from the paths of virtue and wish to retrieve their lost characters.' Such females were a useful source of cheap labour, as seamstresses, laundry maids and servants.

One difficult area was the elderly poor, who could not be punished for not seeking work. There were plenty of almshouses, 22 of them in 1850, but to get a place, the applicant had to have a recommendation from one of its patrons, and the sexes were segregated – as at the workhouses, which were at Clifton for the aged and infirm (though not if they drank), Pennywell Road for the able-bodied, and St George for children. Later purpose-built workhouses were erected at Stapleton, in what became a lunatic asylum, and finally at Southmead. These buildings became the nucleus of Southmead Hospital.

In the 1890s when Charles Booth visited Bristol, investigating the aged poor, he found that more than half the registered paupers in the Bristol Union were 65 or over, who would live on outdoor relief rather than go to one of the workhouses. A vicar giving evidence to the Royal Commission of 1895 said that the elderly Bristolians were 'content to remain half-starved rather than go into the workhouse'.

Then there was the matter of the orphaned children. The scale of the problem is indicated by the thousands of orphans (not all of them from Bristol) who passed through George Muller's homes, the first of which opened in Wilson Street in 1836. Muller, being of his time, made one stipulation, that his orphans must be legitimate, destitute and bereaved of one or both parents by death, in order to be admitted. (Unwanted babies were also farmed out: Amelia Dyer of Long Ashton charged £10 a baby and went to prison for six months when she was caught).

Muller vowed 'never to ask for money from any human being' to fund his great enterprise, and miraculously the donations came in when most needed, thanks to prayer. His

Muller orphan girls learning by rote.

was an enlightened regime at the five 'houses' he eventually built on Ashley Down; he made sure the uniform was not humiliating, his orphans were well fed, they had toys in their playroom, played games and had outings. The limitation of the orphans' education was typical of the age, that the children were equipped for life in a trade if a boy, and in domestic service if a girl, and that intellectual talents were not fostered.

What happened to children who failed to get into an orphanage? They became outcasts, according to a study by the *Bristol Mercury* staff in 1884. In *The Homes Of The Bristol Poor*, they describe 'a boy of nine, dressed in a grotesque costume as a negro minstrel, had his health undermined by being forced every day and night to sing and dance at public houses for the support of the man and woman who had brought him up. He had never gone to school and did not know who his parents were. With his face blackened he was taken sometimes to 40 public houses by the man and woman, who waited out-side to take the money which he got by singing. On an average he earned 3s. 6d. a night and 5s. on Saturday night. He was seized by a School Board officer and sent to Industrial School but was too ill and was sent to the Children's Hospital'. The same report describes street boys who sold matches or paper 'until they crept away to die'.

Victorian Bristolians were not without conscience, but their generosity was selective and the very names of the charitable societies are revealing. These are some listed in 1851: The Prudent Man's Friend Society, the Society For The Reward and Encourage-ment of Female Servants, the Society for the relief of Poor Pious Clergymen, the Society for the Relief and Discharge of Persons Confined for Small Debts, the Bristol and Clifton Mendicity Society, the Grateful Society, which helped with the apprentice-ship of poor boys, and the relieving of poor married lying-in women. It is worth noting

Muller orphan babies in the nursery.

that the Bristol branch of the NSPCA was founded in 1844, nearly half a century before the NPSCC.

The Victorians had a terror of funding vice and laziness, so charity aid went only to the respectable poor. The respectable poor did not have criminal records, they kept their hovels comparatively clean, they did not swear or smoke and above all they did not drink. The theory was that the pinch of poverty would drive the labouring poor to work, and that since destitution was caused by weakness of character, too much help would only encourage fecklessness. The Victorian middle class was also obsessed with stopping the working class drinking, believing that the poor were poor because they drank, rather than that they drank to escape their poverty.

But they were right to view the drink problem seriously, for by the mid-century it was estimated that the poor spent more on drink than on rent. It was easy to do so, for Bristol had an incredible number of pubs, inns, taverns and beer houses; the number grew from 650 in 1840 to 1,250 in the 1870s, serving a population of 162,000. Hotwells Road notoriously had 30 drinking establishments in a quarter of a mile, and the hours of opening were liberal. The temperance movement had began in Bristol but had no real effect until the 1880s.

The one universal source of aid, paid for out of the rates, was the outdoor and indoor relief provided under the Poor Law, amended in 1834 to take over from the patchy parish relief. It was run by Guardians, and designed to make sure that life on outdoor relief (a less than subsistence sum) or in the workhouse was so crushingly bitter that anyone would prefer to work rather than claim it. Private charities were encouraged because they helped to keep down the Poor Law rate charged to each householder.

A Victorian photographer's dream: The Pithay, between Wine Street and Fairfax Street. c.1880.
[Reece Winstone Archive]

Much of central Bristol followed a medieval street pattern. Mary-le-Port Street c. 1890 looking towards St Peter's church. The house on the right was demolished in 1904.
[Reece Winstone Archive]

Without work or charity aid, the only alternative for the poor was crime – mainly theft and prostitution for the women, and burglary, pick-pocketing and mugging for the men. One building in the Redcliffe parish was known to the police as Vermin Farm, a brothel and a lodging house, with ten people to a room. There were sixteen brothels alone in the St James's area, and many prostitutes operated from public houses.

As a result of the Reform Bill, the Bristol police force was set up in 1836; until then the military dealt with disorder. The first police station was in Wine Street and then in the new Bridewell, where the central police station is to this day. Influential Clifton also got its station (now Avon Wildlife Centre) at the foot of Brandon Hill, in 1836. This station had one Inspector, six sergeants and 53 constables, issued with a cape, a greatcoat, a frock coat, trousers, boots, top hat, stock button brushes, rattle and lamp. Fifty cutlasses and 24 handcuffs were kept at the station. By 1841, Bristol had 228 policemen, roughly one per 500 of the population. Among their rules was a ban on conversation with female servants, but they needed something to keep them awake – one constable was found walking asleep. They were paid 16s. a week, and could be hired for private functions; they also got tips for services like catching a pig.

The main task of the new force was to prevent crime by night and day patrols through the city. Walking on set beats at set times, at two and a half miles an hour, they were expected to cover 20 miles per eight-hour day. This was easy enough in quiet districts like Clifton but in the poorer parts of the city it was dangerous, though less so on Thursdays and Fridays when the money for drink ran out before Saturday payday. (No wonder that mid-century there were dozens of pawnbrokers listed in the street directory, in three 'walks' that covered Old Market and Broadmead area, the centre of the city, and Redcliffe and Bedminster.)

One policeman recalled: 'In St Jude and St Philips there were nights when seven different fights were in progress within a distance of 150 yards. Schools for young pickpockets flourished in Tower Lane, soldiers from Horfield barracks challenged police to stand-up fights, and constables could not in safety patrol the Pithay, Silver Street and St Philips Marsh. In Bedminster police and miners engaged in fist fights to settle arguments. Most notorious was Gloucester Lane, St. Philips where in 1870 a policeman was stabbed to death. Magistrates would impose sentences of three months' hard labour for injuring a policeman.'

The most common cause of trouble was drink and in 1874 the Licensing Act required the police to inspect licensed houses, with effect, for together with the temperance movement, the result was that cases of charges for being drunk and disorderly declined, from 4,277 in 1887 to 2,292 in 1895. Other common charges were for petty crimes – shoplifting, burglary, begging, assault and prostitution, though by the late Victorian period there was actually a decrease in reported crime. Street crime apparently went down as street lighting improved.

And the Bristol police force were pioneers: they were the first outside London to set up 24-hour patrols, the first to employ undercover police, and the first to use photographs for criminal records. The story of policing Victorian Bristol was a success story, with crime levels gradually falling as the century progressed. In 1884 they had a coup: they arrested William Donne who was about to make an assassination attempt on the Prince of Wales during a visit to the city.

But a yob culture was also thriving in Victorian Bristol: in 1856 a magistrate remarked that 'Bristol has the unenviable reputation of having within her walls one of the most disorderly sets of youths in England. Stones are continually thrown by boys in public thoroughfares, owing to which many lives have been lost – five at least in Clifton parish only... Ornamental plantations, so placed to benefit the public, are constantly injured and even the branches carried away for firewood. Young thieves assemble in gangs at each end of Park Street, professedly to drag wheels, but really for worse purposes, as proved in many cases. If the police or private individuals complain, they are assailed in gross and indecent language, revolting to all, and especially to females.'

In the 1880s, on Sundays, youths would gather in gangs on the Downs and cause a nuisance by disrupting band performances. Rival Victorian football fans also caused trouble – human nature does not change very much.

Juvenile crime was another problem, until the advent of compulsory and free education. Poor parents could not afford the few pence a week it cost to send their offspring to school, and bands of children roamed the streets begging and stealing, and child prostitution was not uncommon, as the age of consent was raised from 13 to 16 only in 1885.

The punishment for adolescents was often the reformatory, an Industrial School with a military-style regime for younger children. Less harsh was Mary Carpenter's approach. At Red Lodge, which opened as a reformatory for girls in 1854 and at the boys' equivalent in Park Row, she believed in feeding the body and the spirit, helping the children acquire practical skills and allowing them to play games. A kinder regime paid dividends, and heralded a more enlightened attitude to crime and punishment.

So what were the punishments? In 1800 around 200 offences were punishable by death, but in Victoria's reign there were only nine executions of Bristol criminals, all for murder. Transportation had mainly ceased, but sentences for petty crime were hard. Theft of a loaf, or an item of clothing, could result in three to six months in the New Gaol on Cumberland Road or from 1883 in Horfield Gaol, considered a state-of-the-art prison when it opened.

When Victoria came to the throne, the poorer areas of the city were dangerous, despairing places, and crime was endemic but by her death in 1901, Bristol was a much safer city, no longer gripped by fear of crime and riot. But it was not until the slum clearances of the 1930s and the arrival of the welfare state that a serious effort was made to help Bristol's underclass out of poverty.

Snapshots of the Underclass

Police court reports, 1842

Ann Cookley was charged with stealing three pairs of sheets belonging to her mistress, Miss Eliza Glenan, 3, Freeland Place. An assistant from Mr Chilcott's the pawnbroker proved the pledging of the sheets at his shop, and they were identified by Miss Glenan as her property. On the person of the prisoner was found a necklace likewise belonging to the complainant. Committed for trial.

The New Bristol Gaol

It is capable of receiving upwards of 200 prisoners. The governor's house is situated in the centre of four wings of the building and is so arranged that he has a view of the whole of the prison yards without leaving his room. There is a communication between each wing by means of four neat cast iron bridges. The turnkey's lodge, fronting the river, is the entrance, on top of which criminals were formerly executed.

The cells and other apartments are heated by Hazard's patent heating and ventilating apparatus. The prisoners are arranged in ten different classes, each class being cut off from communication with the others. Those committed for felonous practices are compelled to wear a partly-coloured dress. A treadmill is erected for the purpose of raising water for the use of the prisoners. The boundary wall, which is 20 feet high, is built with the variegated marble from St Vincent's Rocks. The whole length of the building is about 358 feet.

Chilcott's Guide, 1846

The execution of Sarah Harriet Thomas, 1849, written by a woman

The victim, a 61 year-old maiden lady of eccentric habits, Miss Jefferies, owned property in Trenchard Street, was found murdered, her head stove in by a stone. Sarah Thomas (18) was her servant. Police hunted her and found her hiding in coal hole; she had stolen a silver tureen and five spoons, a gold watch and sovereigns. She was found guilty and sentenced to death, and efforts to commute the sentence with a petition from the women of Bristol, failed. She was hanged and it was said that 40,000 witnessed the dreadful spectacle.

Letters on the conditions of the working classes of Bristol, from the Examiner's office, 1850

On the parish of St Philips:

As for the houses, they present every appearance of having been built not only for the poor but by the poor, and to have known no other tenants. The greater number are mere shells, often only apparently one brick thick and very many of them have become so ruinous as even here, to be deserted and shut up; while from holes once containing windows, in the tottering walls of others, almost equally dilapidated, the occasional protrusion of a head gives token that they are not yet left without inhabitants.

Crowds lined the streets for philanthropist George Muller's funeral
procession to the Cathedral.

Of one of these crazy tenements, only the lower walls remain … the place was used as
an ash heap for a while but at length an honest hardworking fellow obtained permission
to clear out the rubble and stye a couple of pigs in the remains of a lower front apartment and to stable a horse in those of the back one.

The population of the region under notice appears to consist in very great degree of persons who, being unable to obtain regular employment and thus compelled to tax their
ingenuity to find the means of keeping body and soul together, have either taken up
some petty branch of industry in which the materials cost little and for which there is a
constant demand, others are traders on a small scale, hawking their wares around the
streets, or displaying them in the common room of their dwelling, and so making a pretence of shopkeeping, or lastly they hit on some temporarily successful mode of cloaking
their real occupation – that of beggar.

The personal appearance of the population of this quarter generally is depressing. Dirt,
though more than sufficiently visible, is still perhaps hardly so universally and palpably
apparent as was formerly the case, but a stunted wiry growth and a look of squalid
wretchedness or utter vacancy seems to be hereditary among the people. Here the human
face is shorn of its divinity indeed.

Mary Carpenter on juvenile delinquents in prison, 1853
It is only when the child's soul is touched, when he yields from the heart a willing

obedience, when he can freely cry and exercise his growing powers and apply the knowledge he is gaining in the performance of his daily duties, and to refresh and invigorate his mind with health and intellectual food – that the work of education is really going on. And can this be done in a gaol, even by the kindest and most devoted teacher? The ponderous walls around him crush out his soul as well as confine his body; the high-barred windows exclude all but some small portion of heaven's light and air; his heart is withered by the daily sight of the rod.

Abandoned baby, 1856

On Saturday morning, the body of an infant was discovered, wrapped in an old newspaper, lying in the path from the Observatory to Clifton Down.
Clifton Chronicle

Editorial, *Clifton Chronicle*, 1856

A swarm of beggars now infests Clifton. It needs only a daily walk through the streets to be assaulted by a succession of supplicants for relief, young or old, male or female, whose impertinent importunity is at once disagreeable and disgraceful.

Swindlers, police report 1863

Brigit and Jane Brown, apparently young, gave their ages as 50 and 60, were charged with begging in West Mall. When searched, they had £6 on their persons, begging on the pretence that they were asking for relief for orphans, so that they could emigrate to Australia. Sentenced to one month's hard labour.

Shoplifters, 1863

Three respectably dressed women were charged with stealing nine woollen shawls worth £5. 19s. 6d. from Mr Wyatt draper of 4 and 5 The Mall. They made small purchases and distracted him. They had stolen other things in Wine Street.

A good haul, 1872

A kitchen maid at Clifton Down Hotel was caught stealing bacon, butter, dripping, tea, sugar, knives, chops etc, all concealed under her dress.

Homes of working people in Clifton

I speak of Clifton proper where the contrast between the commodious houses and fine shops of the upper and middle classes and the crampt ill-ventilated dwellings of the working man and petty tradesman which mingle with them, is pitifully apparent. Wellington Place, opposite Prince's Buildings, is shabby and decayed. Almost every family house is let out in several divisions, a whole family occupying the underground kitchen with perhaps a single garret in addition for high rent of 4s. a week. Waterloo Place is equally squalid and the court which winds to it from the Mall buildings is intolerable. There three sets of houses form the main accommodation for Clifton workpeople and far from cheap – Miles Court has a dark unfurnished room for 2s. or 3s. a week.
Letter to Clifton Chronicle, 1857

A domestic missionary describes Bristol vagabonds

Parentage commences early in life, often clandestinely: an infant is born… the child is a pauper, sixpence a week and a loaf being its allowance. The child gets big enough to go to school. It has conceived the idea that it is a place where confinement and whipping are practised. It refuses to go… the child runs in the streets in rags, its head unacquainted with combing, its skin seldom washed and its young ideas about right and wrong very vague. The child arrives at the age when parish pay ceases. It must perforce try to get 'summat'.

The character and living of both parent and child are barriers to its employment for respectable work. If a boy he is sent forth with hearth stone, matches or a 'cadging' bag. With the last he is expected to investigate and overhaul every heap of cinders or rubbish that seems likely to yield anything, from an old shoe-string to a sixpence or a silver spoon. If the child is female, she ventures into the world with matches or pins or blacking or firewood. Growing upwards to adult age, the boy and girl become more irregular, unmanageable and profane.

Report by Rev. J. Shearman, 1853

Great destitution in Hotwells, 1867

Great numbers of poor shivering starving creatures have daily during this inclement weather been relieved by meals of bread and cheese at the Mendicity Office. About 20 cases of very great destitution in the Hotwells are at present under investigation.

Starvation in Clifton, 1870s

The real condition of the working classes of Clifton, is of 350 shipwrights, 300 out of employment, because of stagnation in their trades. They do not like to ask for relief and consequently are nearly starving. They have pledged [pawned] everything valuable, watches, wedding rings etc. Also labourers, sawyers, plasterers, masons, painters, small shopkeepers out of work, so that a quarter of the working population of Clifton is unemployed.

T.H. Clark, curate

Destitution in Clifton

A lady named Andrews and a daughter reside at Sion Hill where until recently, the mother kept a lodging house. Some time ago the furniture was sold by auction and the house was completely stripped of everything in it except one or two old chairs which the poor woman had been obliged to use as a bed. To add to their misfortune, the daughter on Sunday night was delivered of twins … I hope benevolent Clifton will give assistance.

Letter to the Western Daily Press, 1854

Charity at Hotwells

Dinner for the Old People with roast beef, bread, plum pudding was served at 24 tables for 320 guests in the long-disused ballroom at Hotwells. The Entertainment was for poor people over 60 of good character. The ballroom was decorated with flowers, flags and scriptural texts. Though poor, they were cleanly dressed and each was given a

packet of tea and a sugar and a fly home if too feeble to walk.
Clifton Chronicle, 1859

Recipe for charity soup, 1874

Half an ox cheek, sixpennyworth of fresh bones, ten large carrots, twelve turnips, three pounds of potatoes, eighteen leeks or onions, three quarts of split peas. Put the whole of these articles, together with any bones or meat trimmings or cold vegetables there may be in the larder, and any water that meat or poultry has been boiled in, into an iron pot with three gallons of cold water. Put it by the fire to boil up slowly, stir and skim often, and let it simmer for six hours after it boils. Take out all the bones, stir in half an ounce of black pepper and a quarter of a pound of salt. The quantities given will make ten quarts of soup and the cost will be about 5s.

Drunk at a funeral

I have never seen in any town in England or on the Continent so much drunkenness as at the Hotwells in Bristol but on Friday night as I was walking through the Triangle, I was obliged to witness one of the men who was driving a mourning coach so beastly drunk that before descending Park Street, the mourners all left the coach whilst the drunken man was dragged from the box.
Letter to Clifton Chronicle 1875

A Temperance Song

Please sell no more drink to my Father,
It makes him so strange and so wild,
Heed the prayer of my heart-broken Mother,
And pity the poor drunkard's child.

A daring burglary, 1861

The premises of Mr Henry Pearce, proprietor of the Sion Spring Baths at the top of the Zig-Zag were burglarised, entered and robbed. The thieves got first onto the top of an adjacent house and having helped themselves to some dozen boxes of cigars, many of expensive description, a cameo brooch, three snuff boxes and a lot of fancy pebble and agate brooches set in silver, to the value of about £13, they decamped. In order to get out they placed a short ladder on a table which stood underneath the skylight and having ascended the roof once more, made their way to the street and then set off in the direction of Hotwells.

The sentimental Rev. Francis Kilvert sees poverty in central Bristol

As I was sitting in a confectioner's shop between the Drawbridge and College Green, eating a bun, I saw lingering about the door a bare-footed child, a little girl with fair hair tossed and tangled wild. With an arch, eager little face and beautiful wild eyes, large and grey, which looked shyly into the shop and at me with a wistfully beseeching smile.

She wore a poor faded ragged frock and her shapely limbs and tiny delicate beautiful feet were bare and stained with mud and dust… I took her out a bun and I shall never forget the quick happy grateful smile which flashed over her face as she took it and began to eat. She said she was hungry. Poor lamb. I asked her name and she told me, but amid the roar of the street and the bustle of the crowded pavements I could not catch the accents of the childish voice. Never mind, I shall know one day.

Kilvert's Diary, 1874

A brothel in Tower Lane, police report 1877

Sgt. Davis and two police constables raided a house in Tower Lane … In four other bed-rooms I found four other men and four prostitutes in bed or undressing for the purpose of going to bed. There were at the time nine prostitutes working in the house.

Memo from the Chief Constable, 1897

The rod used by police for birching children under 10 should be lighter than that used for other offenders.

The unemployed, letter to *Clifton Chronicle*, 1886

That a firm of contractors came to Bristol to engage 50 men at 17s. to 20s. per week and could only procure 37 speaks for itself. The ranks of the unemployed comprise very largely that numerous body who prefer charity to wages, indolence to honest labour and whose cry is: 'We want no work to do'.

A Pickpocket Punished

William Hollyman, a young sailor, was charged with stealing from the person of Emma Cowlin a purse and 3s. of her money. The prosecution stated that she and her friends were in a saleroom in Castle Street when she noticed the prisoner fumbling with her dress. He at once left the shop and then she, missing her purse, followed him and he was stopped and taken into custody. Sentenced to two months' imprisonment with hard labour.

Bristol Times, 1886

A brutal fellow at the police court

Cornelius Hurley, a rough-looking fellow was charged with assaulting and beating Fanny Amos. The prosecutor stated that she had lived with the defendant in Lamb Street. On Tuesday night, he came home drunk and when they got to their room, he commenced to beat her, he knocked her down, beat her head on the floor, and then kicked her when she was down. She tried to scream but he clutched her mouth and hurt her severely. The blows from the boot gave her a fearful black eye and also injured her throat. The man had already served three months' imprisonment for assaulting her, the chairman said the prisoner had been guilty of a most abominable offence and would be sentenced to six months' imprisonment and he was sorry he could not give him more.

Bristol Times, 1888

A street beggar

At the Bristol Police Court on Monday, Joseph Gregory, 67 years old, was charged with begging. P.C. Rainey deposed to seeing the accused begging in the street at Lawrence Hill. He asked for tobacco and also a halfpenny to make up the cost of his rent and lodging.

Later in the same day, the accused Gregory was reported to have asked for more tobacco and two pence for his night's lodging. Taken in custody, it was found that he had plenty of tobacco on him and 2s. 7d. in copper. He was sentenced to two months' imprisonment with hard labour.

Bristol Observer, 1897

Police report of a charity stunt, 1896, at the Suspension Bridge

A large number of persons assembled in Bridge Valley Road to witness a feat by Mr Zanetto of the People's Palace, Baldwin Street, of catching a turnip, dropped from the bridge, on a tuning fork which he held in his mouth. A number of young ladies were present with boxes collecting money in aid of the Children's Hospital. All passed off orderly and without accident. He caught the fifth turnip which was dropped.

Joyriding, 1900

In Whiteladies Road a pony and trap was stolen and driven furiously at full gallop by four urchins. A police constable jumped on a tram and told the driver: follow that trap, and he did so at full speed, 8–10mph. They were catching up when the horse collapsed from exhaustion.

What the smart bather was wearing in 1887: costumes from Marshall & Snelgrove, Oxford Street, London.

5 – Leisure: The Victorians enjoy themselves

LIKE EVERYTHING ELSE IN VICTORIAN BRISTOL, how you spent your leisure depended on what social class you belonged to. One can imagine Victorian society in Bristol as a pyramid of clubs, with the Merchant Venturers at the top, and the Working Men's Clubs at the bottom.

Inside the pyramid were gentlemen's clubs, ladies' charities, societies for the promotion, prevention and abolition of things, church groups, chapel groups, Sunday schools, cultural and educational clubs, hobbies and sporting clubs, military volunteers, missions, and for the working class most of these activities took place in the context of the church or chapel, or the pub.

There was a form of cultural apartheid: the middle classes went to the Princes Theatre and the Victoria Rooms for their entertainment, the working classes went to the Theatre Royal and the Empire music hall. The middle classes used private lending libraries, the working class used the public libraries.

In religion, schools, shops, housing, education and leisure, culture all ran on these parallel tracks, and about the only place where the classes mixed was on the playing fields, where football and cricket had democratised the players.

Leisure was both a blessing and a problem. For low-paid blue collar workers, there was too little of it. They worked 12 hour days, 6am to 6pm, six days a week. For middle-class women with several servants, and daughters at home waiting to get married, the problem was too much leisure in a world circumscribed by rules about what a lady might and might not do.

So how did Victorian Bristolians have fun? A lot of entertainment went on in the streets. Musicians, jugglers, strong men, conjurers, circus performers, singers, actors, minstrels, dancers, hurdy-gurdy men, would tour the city hoping to attract an audience and a few pennies in a hat. Letters from Disgusted of Clifton frequently complained of the noise and mess caused by these itinerant entertainers.

The lower classes took their pleasures out of doors, being vigorous walkers and keen picnickers, and the city's acquisition of the Downs made it the focus of outdoor entertainment from 1861 on. Bristol was well off for public parks; as early as 1847 the citizens could enjoy their spare time on Queen Square, Portland Square, College Green and Brandon Hill.

Parades and processions, often in costume, through the streets, and in particular military displays, attracted huge crowds, and there was bound to be one big event every weekend. Sunday Band concerts on the Downs were so popular that crowds of 20,000 were

Zebi, presented to the Zoo by the Maharajah
of Mysore in 1868, became a popular
character who lived until 1909.
Here he is with keeper Jim Rawlings.

common. Cliftonians were not entirely happy about it – one 1860s correspondent to the *Clifton Chronicle* wrote that the suburb had become 'quite vulgar since the tagrag of Bristol have taken so much resort to it'.

Another outdoor venue which drew the crowds was the Zoo, which opened in 1836. At first it had to rely on popular entertainment, rather than the animals, for revenue, and the Zoo gardens were used for all kinds of events, from balloon ascents, boat launches in the lake, carnivals, exhibition lacrosse, golf and tennis matches, brass band contests, tightrope walking, dog shows and bicycle races.

In 1855, an attraction was gymnastics with Master Drouet, the unrivalled Lilliputian clog dancer, and Signor Gomez, the modern Sampson. This was the year the Siege of Delhi was re-enacted. Right up to Edwardian times, a famous Zoo carnival was held every summer. For the centenary of the Sunday Schools in 1880, 16,000 children walked in procession with 2,000 teachers to the Zoo to spend a day there.

The Victoria Rooms in their early years. Dickens and Oscar Wilde would wow audiences here.

Industrial exhibitions and horticultural and farm shows drew enormous audiences. Outings on trams and steamers and bicycles came later in the century; the works or Sunday School outing was a big feature in the calendar of any firm or social or church club. Later on, excursions by train to the seaside were highly popular, and the very first touring caravan was built in Bristol in 1883, by the Bristol Wagon Works. It still survives and can be seen in the Industrial Museum.

The middle and upper classes tended to seek their entertainment more privately, at home, with dinner parties, tennis parties, soirées and balls, theatrical entertainments, and in the summer, charity garden parties. Middle-class women denied the opportunity of working, had to fill their hours, and they did it planning social events and making things to sell for their pet charity at the endless fêtes and bazaars.

It was with them in mind that the Victoria Rooms and the Princes Theatre were built as places of respectable entertainment. The Victoria Rooms, designed by architect Charles Dyer, and one of Bristol's most handsome public buildings, had its foundation stone laid in 1838. It was paid for by public subscription and its design was plainly for the convenience of carriage-owning Clifton. The carriages would drop their passengers under the Corinthian portico, and the servants would take the carriages round to the back, and wait for their masters in the tiny servants' hall.

Inside, the Rooms were laid out for a variety of events; there was an organ for concerts, a stage, rooms in which to hold balls, lectures, bazaars and conferences – the first public meeting there was of the Royal Agricultural Society – but mainly the Victoria Rooms were a venue for entertainments by famous figures of the day and talks on anything from mesmerism and telephonic communication to world peace and beekeeping.

An instant sell-out was a visit by Charles Dickens's theatre company in 1851; Adelina Patti and Jenny Lind performed there, Oscar Wilde lectured on aesthetics, there was Maskelyne and Coote's Magic Show and Lola Montez, exotic singer, and Mrs Shaw, the

The Tivoli Palace of Varieties, Broadmead, in 1900.

Whistling Lady. Magic lantern shows were also popular and this was one of the first buildings in Bristol to be electrically lit.

Dickens gave two readings in May, 1866 with excerpts from *Nicholas Nickleby*, *David Copperfield*, and *Pickwick Papers*. The press reported: 'it is superfluous to say that a great intellectual treat was afforded and that Mr Dickens moved his hearers to laughter and Anon melted them to tears as he graphically delineated the creations of his genius.'

The Princes Theatre in Park Row, originally named the New Theatre Royal to make its point, was built as a better-class venue for the middle classes than the old gaff, the old Theatre Royal, which for most of the Victorian period struggled to stay running. The New Theatre Royal was opened in 1867 with the aim of putting on popular, respectable, slightly up-market entertainment, plays and opera, and as at the Victoria Rooms, ticket prices were high, in order to discourage the riff-raff. All the famous names of the day appeared there, Ellen Terry, Henry Irving, Sarah Bernhardt, Lily Langtry; the Savoy Opera; the Carl Rosa visited, and the panto was so famous that even George Bernard Shaw recommended it. Drama ranged from light comedy and farce to Shakespeare and the latest play by Ibsen. Sadly this impressive theatre was completely destroyed in the Blitz.

The cynical *Lesser Columbus*, a waspish observer of the 1893 Bristol scene, said:

> The Princes Theatre is the fashionable playhouse of Bristol and is a handsome enough edifice. The auditorium is vast and comfortable. It is in a way a monopoly, for the old Theatre Royal is mostly given over to the common or garden order of imbecile melodrama and appeals eloquently to those who glory vociferously in the vanquishing of the villain and who return home and give vent to their pent-up feelings in beating their wives.

He claimed that the Theatre Royal dressing rooms were 'dirty beyond all cleansing, rotten beyond all repair and sans pretence to even indecent sanitary arrangements.'

Organ grinders were part of Bristol's colourful street life in the 1850s. [Bristol Record Office]

Between 1837 and 1901, the Theatre Royal had a very chequered existence. In the 1840s there were operas, visits from the Female American Serenaders and Madame Wharton's Walhalla Exhibition, interspersed with panto like Harlequin Gobbledy in 1843, the story of Lady Godiva, and the odd Shakespeare production with water effects and live animals; Miss Fanny Bennett played Hamlet in 1855, there was Bluebeard in 1864, *The Field of The Cloth of Gold* in 1868, and Mr Osgood the Chimney Sweep from Redland Green.

The building was decaying, and the quality of the plays was questionable, though there was an improvement in the 1880s when Irving and Terry appeared in *The Merchant of Venice*; a great hit was *Called Back*, a psychological melodrama adapted from the best-selling novel by Hugh Fargus, a Bristol auctioneer. Lily Langtry appeared in *A Young Tramp*, and Clara Butt sang there in 1887. Sarah Bernhardt produced *La Dame Aux Camelias* in 1895, and in 1898 Mrs Patrick Campbell and Gerald du Maurier appeared in Sullivan's opera *The Emerald Isle*.

But respectable people and above all women stayed away – King Street was rough and dangerous. There was severe competition from musical halls like the Alhambra (1870), The People's Palace in Baldwin Street (1892), and The Empire in Old Market (1893). Here Bristolians could see the top London comedians like Harry Tate, Marie Lloyd, George Robey, Little Tich, or the young Chaplin, as well as Graeco-Roman wrestling, the white-eyed musical Kaffir, Charles Noisee, the living skeleton, Don Everest and his

Clifton Rugby Club, founded in 1872.

troupe of monkey gymnasts, Miss Bessie Wentworth, female coon impersonator, and Miss Effie White, fire dancer, but it was at the Palace that the greatest rival to live entertainment was launched in 1896, with a cinematography exhibition by the Lumiere Brothers.

On the music scene, Victorian Bristol had hundreds of music groups of all kinds; every church and chapel had its choir and its band, there were glee societies and dozens of orchestras, amateur and professional, ladies' choruses, and male voice choirs not to mention the venerable Madrigal Society founded in 1837. Music festivals dated back to 1727, and in 1872, a triennial festival was established. All these musicians needed somewhere to perform. The need for a purpose-built concert hall led to the building of the Colston Hall in 1867. The cost, £40,000, was met by the Colston Hall Company shareholders, the major ones being Conrad Finzel, George Thomas, Robert Charleton and Henry Overton Wills.

The great columned main concert hall with its Willis organ held 2,500 people seated and 6,000 standing, and the two other halls held 700 and 400. This building became the centre of musical life in Victorian Bristol. When it burned down in the great fire of 1898, there was no question that it should not be rebuilt, and the next Colston Hall opened in 1900 with a grand reception and a ball attended by 1,000 guests. This was the building that was destroyed by fire once again, in 1945.

At the other end of the scale there were small halls all over the city, like the Albert Hall in Hotwells, where local entertainments could take place, clubs could meet, games could be played; the church hall was vital to social life. This was where the Boys' Brigade met, or the Women's Bright Hour, where the spelling bee or the sewing and cookery classes took place. The middle classes were anxious to encourage such activities because they kept the working classes out of the pub, the other refuge from cramped and sub-standard housing.

Working men's clubs always had a games room with table tennis, billiards, and so on,

Clifton Bicycle Club on the Downs, 1886. [Reece Winstone Archive]

and enlightened employers provided facilities for sport by the end of the century. The YMCA opened its first branch in 1883 with provision for 'physical recreation'.

Sport was another way of keeping men away from the drink, but in the early half of Victoria's reign, organised games were not the rule, and there were few public spaces set aside for sport, apart from the Downs. It took the arrival of Clifton College and schools that imitated it, to establish the idea of organised games and team spirit. Equipment became cheaper and interest was roused by the local press printing reports and results, and as the century progressed more space was put aside for pitches. But board schools were not generally built with anything more than a gym indoors and an asphalt playground where only drill could take place.

The earliest sports club was Clifton Cricket Club, founded in 1819; they played on the Downs from 1837 to 1930. Bedminster was another early club, founded in 1847. The great sporting hero was of course W.G. Grace, who in 1895 was given a banquet at the Victoria Rooms, to celebrate his 100th century. A very bad poem was printed on the menu:

When sixties saw your rise, W.G,
Cheers were mingled with surprise, W.G.
Time, it seems, has made some blunder,
Still the plaudits sound like thunder,
We've forgotten how to wonder, W.G.

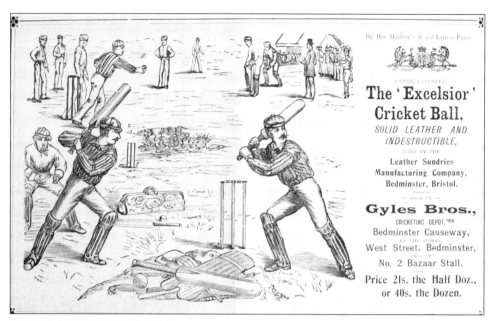

The 'Excelsior'
Cricket Ball,
*SOLID LEATHER AND
INDESTRUCTIBLE,*
MADE BY THE
Leather Sundries
Manufacturing Company,
Bedminster, Bristol.
— SOLD BY —
Gyles Bros.,
CRICKETING DEPOT,
Bedminster Causeway,
AT THE WORKS,
West Street, Bedminster,
AND AT
No. 2 Bazaar Stall.
Price 21s. the Half Doz.,
or 40s. the Dozen.

Bristol and Gloucestershire folk hero: W.G. Grace, captain of England cricket team.

Rugby was introduced to Bristol by Clifton College, and the earliest club, one of the first in the country, was Clifton, founded in 1872, followed by Bristol Rugby Club in 1888. By 1875 Clifton had its first England cap. It was a rough game, often played 20 a side, and occasionally players died from their injuries. W.G. Grace played a few times but found it too rough for him. Clifton was the first team in the country to play a match under artificial lights – in 1881, at Weston-super-Mare, to a crowd of over 4,000.

Organised football in the city was unknown until Clifton and Warmley both formed clubs in 1882. Other districts soon followed suit, so that the game became the one place where the different classes played together, though Warmley followers said they found the Clifton fans 'too snooty'. The Western League was started in 1892 and professional football arrived in 1897. Five clubs turned professional but only Bristol City and Bristol Rovers survived.

Sports which women could enjoy became popular: they entered archery contests at the Zoo, played tennis at the Clifton Tennis Club, founded in 1881, and golf – the Bristol and Clifton Golf Club was established in 1891, when they began to lay out their course at Failand. Cycling was a Victorian passion and in 1889 a cycling track was opened at the County Ground, which had opened the previous year. The first rowing club was the

The Royal West of England Academy, as originally built with entrance at first-floor level.

Bristol Ariel, formed in 1870, while swimming was still confined to lakes and the New Cut and the Floating Harbour, or the private pools like the Victoria Baths, Clifton, which opened in 1850.

What was the city doing to provide leisure facilities? The answer is not much: a terror of offending the ratepayers by putting up the rates made municipal provision of swimming pools, tennis courts, libraries, a museum and art gallery, a controversial move, and rich patrons like the Wills family were relied on to fill the gaps.

There were private museums and galleries but they had peculiar collections, as the list of items in the Bristol Institution reveals: the building at the bottom of Park Street held an astronomical clock, meteorological instruments, suits of armour, a bust of Byron, two marine models, a mummy, a Burmese idol, sepulchral urns, fossils, the skeleton of an elephant, aquatic birds, an insect cabinet and various reptiles.

In its art collection, according to the *Bristol Times* of 1842, the Institution had an unequalled Rembrandt and two Raphaels amongst a 'rare assemblage of choice paintings in condition so fine, of originality so unquestionable as is rarely or ever met with except in a few royal and public galleries'. But it cost 2s. to get in, a price way beyond the working man. The plans for a free City Art Gallery and Museum came only at the very end of Victoria's reign and then only thanks to the generosity of Sir William Wills.

With improvement in literacy, libraries became another place to spend leisure time, and they were popular thanks to the Victorian passion for self-improvement, but here again there was a class divide. The working classes had to rely on libraries provided by church or chapel, while the middle classes, who feared germs, used private lending libraries, and there were dozens of these. In the 1880s, Massingham's Lending Library claimed to have 50,000 volumes at its Regent Street Clifton premises, and local residents resisted the establishment of a public library. The Public Libraries Act was passed in 1874, and the Corporation then took full responsibility. The King Street library became open to the general public and the first branch library at St Philips opened in 1894; by 1899 there were seven branches.

At the beginning of the nineteenth century use of leisure time had been totally unorganised; by 1900, Bristol was awash with leisure and entertainment facilities. Improved literacy rates, improved health, greater wealth and shorter working hours were the motors behind all this activity, and by the end of the century, leisure, sporting and cultural events involved many thousands of Bristolians of every class, every weekend. Victorians believed in *mens sana in sano corpore*; it was your duty to enjoy yourself.

Snapshots of Leisure

Exhibition at the Horticultural Rooms, Park Street

In addition to the extensive and valuable collection of Paintings, Models, Specimens of Natural History and Manufactures, Articles of Vertu etc. etc., a SPLENDID MECHANICORAMA is exhibited with views of Rising Sun and Bay of Naples. The Views are accomplished by a variety of interesting and appropriate MECHANICAL FIGURES.

LAUGHING GAS EVERY EVENING: The introduction of laughing gas for Ladies alone having proved so attractive and satisfactory, arrangements are made to have it repeated on Wednesday and Friday next at one; it will be administered by a lady and none but ladies will be admitted to the room.
Bristol Times, 1842

Great Exhibition Fever

As the closing date of October 11 drew near, thousands panicked into taking one of their last chances to visit the marvel of the age, by leaving at 6.39am from Temple Meads for the capital. Numbers far in excess of the GWR's expectation besieged the station, battling for cheap tickets and the 16 scheduled carriages became hopelessly insufficient. Another dozen were borrowed from an obliging Midland Railway but although 2,000 people got away, another 700 were left behind at Bristol, venting their disappointment milling around the station, halting all other operations.
Bristol Journal, September 1851

Exterior of the New Theatre Royal (later renamed The Princes) on Park Row. [*Illustrated London News*, Christmas, 1869: Bristol University Theatre Collection]

A Dingy Old Place

It is very seldom that we visit the Bristol Theatre, for, excepting a star now and then, there is nothing to tempt one to leave a comfortable fireside for a dingy old place, every year getting more and more gloomy, scenery every inch of which is familiar and tired withal, property that is the property of moths, boxes clear of occupants and the pit the forlorn hope of an orange-seller woman, the gallery noisy.

Bristol Journal, 1851

The handing over of the Downs to the Corporation in 1861

The beautiful scenery of the Avon, the pure fresh air from the distant sea, know no caste. They are free to be enjoyed by the most lowly. The poor man may watch the white-winged craft come up the winding Avon, he may see the sun descending in all its gorgeous magnificence, he may contemplate the thousand tints of Leigh Woods.

Editorial in the Bristol Mirror, 1861

The Catastrophe Last Night

Last night a calamity of appalling magnitude took place at the New Theatre Royal, Park Row, as the doors were about to be opened to admit the public … considerable expectations being formed as to the new pantomime.

As the hour of opening drew near, the street was so massed that it was very evident that there could not be room for more than a fraction of those who wished to be admitted. The effect of this conviction, coupled with the desperate determination not to lose one's chance of seeing the performance, caused too frightful a crush towards the avenue leading off the street towards the pit and gallery doors of the entrance, that cries of distress were got up from within the avenue, which at first were disregarded, or only incited those outside to crush in more desperately … Those nearest the doors thus struggled to get out, and those outside to get in; and at the meeting of the two tides was literally fatal, and to a fearful extent. Eighteen lives were lost in the occasion, and a multiplicity of injuries inflicted … The panic was so sudden, and the evil effects of it so immediately precipitated, that of those in the Theatre – for it was filled almost as soon as the doors were opened – by far the greater number were unaware of anything wrong, the work of death was still going on.

Western Daily Press, December 27, 1869

Charles Dickens's farewell reading at the Victoria Rooms

Precisely at 8 o'clock Mr. Dickens stepped onto the platform. His appearance did not awaken that prolonged applause which often greets a favourite or well-known artist but the earnest and continued gaze directed to him from every part of the room… Without introduction of any sort, he gave the barest announcement of his theme and proceeded to narrate the personal history of David Copperfield. At first he took his hearers to the picturesque and humble home of old Pegotty and described the quaint interior… The scene in which David introduces Steerforth afforded Mr Dickens a fine opportunity for displaying the vast resources as a delineator of character. Perhaps the author's greatest triumphs were his recitals of the shipwreck scene and the recognition of Pegotty on the steps of St Martin's Church.

Bristol Times and Mirror, 1869

Anti-social Behaviour

Dear Sir, I am subjected each evening on the beautiful Clifton Downs by a horde of half-clad Italian organ boys, who possessed of monkeys, guinea-pigs etc., pertinaciously harass each person … of course the police are never in sight.

Letter to the Clifton Chronicle, 1864

At the Gentlemen's Club – A badly behaved baronet

An apology, in justice to my friend (who brought me in) and other members of your Club, I think it my bounden duty to inform you that I, as an after dinner joke, mutilated a coat in the lavatory, which I hardly need say, I now regret having done so and beg herewith to tend my sincere apologies to the owner.

Clifton Club minutes, 1888

A Clifton College schoolboy's summer vacation

Visited all the Swimming Baths within reach, bought flies for fishing in the lakes, played croquet and lawn tennis, went by steam from Cumberland Basin to Hotwells, visited the museum and played cricket everywhere and with everybody including girls. My holiday task: books read, *Tales Of All Countries*, *Pickwick*, *Boys Own Paper*, *Lothair*, *Thackeray's Burlesques*, *Last Days of Pompeii*, *Dropped From The Clouds*, *The Mysterious Island*, and *Miller's Chemistry*.

Diary of a Fag, by Francis Newbolt, brother of the poet Henry, 1879

Harry Bow enjoys himself

I turned up at Lee's (the undertaker) just after 8am to look for biz, there was a job but

Photography was a novel, and expensive, middle-class pursuit.

The Empire Theatre, Old Market Street, pen-and-ink drawing by F.G. Lewin. [*Bristol Times and Mirror*]

I wasn't needed and the boss gave me 6d, instead. He also gave I an order to do him two more pictures of his funeral corteges, like he got now, good iron. Came home to dinner and had a jaw and a smoke with Fred. In afternoon I starts off again, down to Hotwells by the Rocks Railway, a nigger troupe was performing before a crowd, then up over Observatory Hill, along the promenade and the Downs. Twas such a fine day and looked a real treat and plenty of folks about. Came back through Clifton to the Red Lodge, seen my pals there George and Mrs Stevens etc., had tea and a warble with them, and twas Mrs Moore's birthday so we drank her health. I left and posted a letter to Tom and a fine moonlight night twas, and home to doss.

Harry Bow's diary, March 1893. He was an undertaker's pall-bearer.

An elegant occasion

A ball at Manilla Hall, home of Mrs William Miles, was the most elegant ever given in Clifton. Every arrangement was made which could conduce to the beauty of the scene and the enjoyment of the guests. Dancing to Taylor's admirable quadrille band began at 10.30, supper at 11.30 and dancing until 4. The hall was decorated with banners and garlands of flowers; the libraries were appropriated for dancing and decorated in the same style and the conservatory was lit by innumerable lamps among the rare and exotic plants.

Clifton Chronicle, 1880

An unpopular proposal to extend trams to Clifton

Poor people do not walk about on Clifton streets, and now here are those money-making plebeians of Bristol talking of running tramcars through our beautiful lordly Clifton … Why is this to be? Why must common people be allowed to walk about here? They should stay in their own homes. They would feel more comfortable among their own houses and streets than here. The policemen should stop it. Let them take the tram to Hotwells and then use the Lift (the Rocks Railway).
Clifton Chronicle, 1880

A Victorian looks back at life in the 1890s

The Horsefair, to the young was a wonderful place and Wombwell's Menagerie sometimes stayed there for long periods, and what with boxing booths and side shows it was paradise to me. Captain Cardona went into the cage with man-eating lions, with two men placed outside ready with hot iron bars to push at the lions if needed for the tamer's protection. Quite an old Negro used to perform some wonderful feats of strength on a piece of waste ground, breaking copper by expanding his biceps was one of them and another was to place a 56lb weight on a piece of wood held in his teeth and then throw it over his head.
W. H. Potter

Supper Menu at an Aesthetic Ball at the Victoria Rooms, January 1886

Saumon à la Royale, Game Pies, Boar's Head, Tongues, Turkey à la Royale, Ham, Roast Turkeys, Mayonnaise de Homard, Fillets de Sole en aspic, Braised peafowl pie, Lamb cutlets en aspic, Roast Pheasant, Lamb Cutlets à la Belle Vue aux Truffles, Plovers and Snipe, Black game, Raised Pigeon Pie, Pate de foie gras en Aspic, Rouelle de veau, roast chickens, Aspic de petits Oiseaux, Gallantine de Poulet, Boeuf bouilli aux natural, Victoria Cake, Savoy cake, Compote de fruits, Maraschino Bavarian cream, Swiss ice pudding, wine jelly, noyeau jelly, Lemon cream, Maraschino jelly, Trifles, Compote d'orange, Genoese pastry, Charlotte Russe, Vanilla cream, Pineapple cream, French pastry, Maids of Honour.

Harry Bow goes to the Zoo

I went round by the lake and seen a man climb up on a wire over the water with pole in hand. He walked along it and either by accident or design, tumbled off. Then I goes on tour in all the houses, seeing the various animals. I strolls about, has smokes, and a lot of nice dotlets were dancing to the band, playing kiss in the ring. When it got dark they had a display of fireworks and sent up a balloon. It finished off with the words Success To Forestry and a treat it was indeed.
Harry Bow's Diary, 1893

The Bristol Orpheus Glee Society sings to the Queen in 1895

A special train was provided to convey the members to Windsor where the choir assembled with Mr Riseley their conductor, on a platform constructed in St George's Hall. They had to remain standing for the whole of their concert and no supports were provided for their music – they had their loyalty to sustain them. The programme lasted

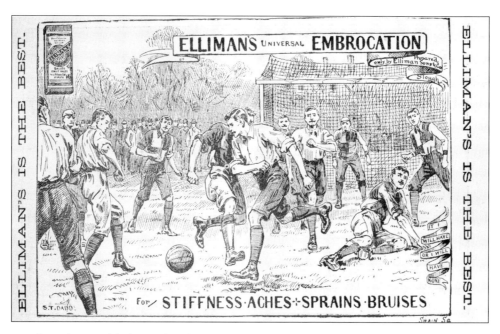

nearly an hour, with the National Anthem arranged by Riseley, Tom Cooke's *Strike The Lyre*, Sullivan's *The Long Day Closes*, Cooke's *Hohenlinden*, two trifles from the pen of Mr C. Lee Williams, organist of Gloucester cathedral, *Ossian's Hymn To The Sun*, Viotta's *The Dying Child*, *O Mistress Mine*, and *Stars of the Summer Night*. There were 32 in the audience and Her Majesty was in an armchair with a small table by her. She had a specially prepared programme printed on art paper, ornamented with sketches, the pages having handsome borders in gold and colours drawn by hand.

The Queen said what she had heard was most charming and delightful and said that she had never heard such delightful singing at Windsor before. After the National Anthem, the Queen, supported by an Indian servant, quitted the hall.

A Saturday Pop at the Colston Hall

While the performance is proceeding, we cannot help noticing various idiosyncrasies. Here may be seen a being pertaining to the female gender, wildly flourishing a pocket handkerchief in the endeavour to cool herself … the continual conversation of a boy and a girl near us is a great nuisance. Why people should come to a concert – presumably to hear the performance – and keep up a chatter, we cannot imagine. From the other gallery comes a sound in the ppp parts of the cracking of nuts which is rather disturbing. Some consider themselves musicians of no small ability and not content with listening, endeavour to beat time to the piece being performed – evidently to their own entire satisfaction. *Letter to the Western Daily Press, 1886*

Bristol's first display of Moving Pictures, 1895

The programme at the Tivoli Music Hall, Broadmead, consisted of scenes in a blacksmith's shop, a wrestling match between a man and a dog, a burlesque boxing match, a

Spanish dance, the execution of Mary Queen of Scots, the burning of Joan of Arc and a re-enactment of the first dental extraction under gas. Later in the week they added footage of the Prince of Wales's horse Persimmon winning the Derby. The *Western Daily Press* commented: 'The animatograph, as the invention has been termed, has certainly a future before it and although the productions show room for improvement they were such as to delight the large audience.'

Advice to ladies using the Victoria Swimming Baths

[The pool opened, for men only, in 1850]

If the heavy flannel dress usual in the sea is adopted, which impedes all freedom of motion in the water, the bath for ladies can never become popular. Let the dress consist of drawers reaching from the waist to the knees and of a tight fitting Garibaldi jacket or vest fastened at the waist, and without sleeves, close round the neck to adapt it better for forward movement. It may have a short skirt but not full. Let these be of the lightest flannel or serge so as to retain as little water as possible.

Letter to Clifton Chronicle, 1871

A Fancy Dress football match at Greenway Bush Lane, Captain Ally Sloper *v.* Lady Muldoon

Fancy dresses included Bluejacket, sweep, cricketer, drayman, fireman, Mrs Stag's Cabbage, policeman, postman, Red Indian, Jack Tar and several natives of Africa. In the 1894-95 football season, the Ladies' Football Team came to Bristol to put on a match at Greenway Bush Lane in front of 2,000 spectators. Unfortunately two of the ladies were indisposed so two young men went in goal and the Blues beat the Reds 5–1.

From the Rules of The Clifton Cycling Club, 1878

The Club will pay the expense of any member who prosecutes a person for stone or cap throwing or other mischievous interference with bicyclists.

A Football Song

Once more on the Football Ground
Let our ringing cheers resound,
For the boys well-known both far and near,
They're the heroes of today
And the game they love to play
Is to Bristol City Sportsmen ever dear.

Chorus:
Play up, Bristol City, add more glory to your name,
You're the Champions of the West,
And are equal to the best
At the jolly old Association game.

Bristol City Supporters' song, 1895
(sung to the tune of *Tramp, tramp, tramp, the boys are marching)*

Football hooligans, 1890s

If the disgraceful scenes witnessed at Kingsweston on Saturday are repeated, the days of Association Football in this neighbourhood at least as far as respectable people are concerned, are numbered. Here was a case in which a man committed a flagrant breach of the rules and was rightly ordered off the field, whereupon the bulk of the spectators behaved in what was nothing short of a brutal manner. Not content with yelling and using language of a disgusting character, they swarmed upon the field at half time to hustle the referee. We are almost inclined to wish that someone had really assaulted him and then the magistrates at Lawford's Gate would have had an opportunity of making an example of these cowardly blackguards. Was this a sport for gentlemen?
Comment in Bristol Mirror

***Lesser Columbus* on W.G. Grace, 1893**

He is as much a national feature as the climate but a good deal more reliable. He devotes what time he can spare apart from killing of bowlers to the doctoring of frail humanity and is a familiar figure on Bristol streets where illness most does congregate. He is big, burly, bronzed and bearded, the essence of good humour, geniality and gentlemanliness.

The Clifton College Cricket XI beats Cheltenham in the 1880s

The game was played away and news of the victory preceded them. They were met near the college by the Sergeant … a little further on the head of school and another prefect were standing at a corner to prepare the way. As they turned the corner, the team saw the assembled school ready to pay homage. A phalanx of boys 15 deep stretched across the wide road – over 600 of them; one tremendous yell burst from their throats and then an outburst of continuous cheering lasted many minutes. The name of each member of the team was shouted and cheered, including the scorer.

Cricket at Clifton High School, in the 1890s, by the wicket keeper for the First XI

When I appeared in pads, which I always wore at home, I was told that I could not use them as they were not considered proper for ladies. We played hockey in long skirts six inches from the ground, wore hard hats and stiff starched collars and cuffs that sometimes shot off your wrists and down the stick.

Amusement for working men

The Committee are in a position to offer a great variety of amusement for the working classes, viz, one splendid billiard table full-sized and one smaller table, also other games such as chess, draughts, dominoes etc. The Committee have also introduced a Musical Evening once a week for the benefit of young members as an inducement to join the club without having to seek amusement at the public houses. The public is requested to donate library books. Gambling is strictly forbidden.
Report on the Working Men's Club and Institute, Victoria Street, Clifton, 1890-91

A Grand Bazaar at the Victoria Rooms 1901

A set of beautiful Living Pictures (beautifully lit by coloured electric lamps) will (DV) be given by the Church of St Paul Clifton on behalf of the new church of the poor parish of St Michael with Angels, Bedminster, in the Victoria Rooms, October 17–19. The opening ceremony will be performed by Lady Doreen Long, with concerts, conjurer, dramatic performances, a Professor of Phrenology, Mandoline Band, shooting gallery, picturesque stalls, and good refreshments.

Queen Victoria visits Bristol, November 1899

Through the combined efforts of the Reception Committee and the inhabitants, every thoroughfare through which the Queen had to pass presented a continuous line of chaste ornamentation. To mention merely one example, from each side of the High Street were suspended golden eagles carrying laurel wreaths and supporting garlands of flowers; whilst in Corn and Clare Streets crimson Venetian masts bore Imperial crowns and supported trophies of flowers, flags and monograms.

Latimer's Annals of Bristol

Fred Beacham of Hotwells sees the Queen, 1899

The Queen visited Bristol to open the Victoria Hospital [at the top of Blackboy Hill, later a maternity hospital] and all the schools were congregated together from the top of Pembroke Road right to the top of Durdham Down. Hotwells Scouts and Board School were selected to head the procession, I was chosen to carry the standard, and we all marched up to Durdham Down. All the schools went on a stand, and were conducted by George Riseley, who was the organist at the Colston Hall. I had to go out in front with the banner – the Union Jack. As the Queen came by, we had to dip the banner in salute to her. Everyone thought to see the Queen go by with a crown but she was a miserable looking woman with a tiny hat on her head.

Poem for the Queen's Visit, 1899, by Mr. G. Gulliver, professor of music

Welcome now, O Gracious Queen,
Thou art so good and just and true,
All thy subjects' love I ween,
Binds them to a Queen like you.
May our God's most gracious love
Shine on them in brightest sheen,
And the Holy Ghost above,
Shed its blessing on our Queen.

Clifton Chronicle, November 29, 1899

overleaf : High Street from Bristol Bridge c.1890. [Reece Winstone Archive]

6 – Getting around

I<small>T IS HARD TO APPRECIATE</small> how difficult it was to get around Bristol at the beginning of Victoria's reign.

If you were wealthy and could afford your own stable, carriage, horse, and groom, there was no problem, apart from the terrible rutted state of the roads. Moderately well-off people could afford to hire a carriage – but they had to send a servant or walk to the premises of the hirer, or to one of the cab stands dotted throughout the city. If you lived near the Docks, you could hire a wherry for a sixpenny ride into the heart of the city. The Avon, the Floating Harbour and the New Cut all had to be crossed by ferry.

Travel by horse and carriage to and from Bristol was expensive in 1837; the city was ringed with 15 turnpikes, and tolls had to be paid. The tolls did not disappear until 1867. If you needed to travel outside Bristol, and you did not own a horse, you could either pay for a place on a carrier's cart, or get the stage coach, which took hours if not days to reach its destination. The rest of Bristol's citizens who wanted to visit outlying villages had to hitch a lift on a tradesman's cart, or walk – there was no alternative. In 1837, Brunel's Great Western Railway had been laid only as far as Didcot, and the Suspension Bridge had only one abutment built, on the Leigh Woods side, and getting to Bristol from north Somerset meant going the long way round by road.

And walking was not easy, for only the streets in central Bristol had pavements, generally made from wood blocks. The roads were made from limestone from the Black Rock quarry in the Avon Gorge, a stone which powdered easily, forming clouds of dust in summer, and ditches full of water in winter. Add to this the mud and rubbish which piled up in a bank each side of the road, and was only cleared if residents paid to have it privately removed, and the dim sporadic gas lighting, and walking was a hazardous and filthy exercise.

So it is no wonder that two men were particularly honoured by Bristolians: Isambard Kingdom Brunel who provided a railway, and Sir George White who provided the tram service. Both men revolutionised communications: Brunel opened Bristol to the world, while White transformed city living with his tram system, which allowed citizens to choose where they lived and worked.

Did Bristol really appreciate Brunel's vision and the gifts that his engineering genius brought? Until the arrival of the Great Western Railway, which opened up trade and travel to London and the West country, Bristol had relied on water routes to get goods distributed; now a trip which took six days by sea to London took a few hours by train. Those who had to travel to London in the uncomfortable and dangerous stage coach (the

Brunel's first great ocean liner, the ss *Great Western*, built in Bristol in 1837.

last Bristol to London service ran in 1843) could now travel in comparative comfort, if they went first class. The third class had to travel early or late, in dangerous trucks with open sides, unprotected from the weather until 1845, and their journey could take up to 10 hours.

The revolutionary great ships that Brunel built in Bristol, the *Great Western* (1837) and the *Great Britain* (1843), were Bristol's chance to corner mail, passenger and freight trade to America and Australia. The prestige and fame that Brunel brought Bristol was inestimable – the image was of a city at the cutting edge of engineering progress.

But the big new ships had to navigate the winding Avon, or wait in King Road while people and goods were brought to them; although Brunel was allowed to make some improvements to the city docks, it was clear that the new big steamships spelled Bristol's doom unless the city dock locks were widened to receive them, or a new dock was built at Portishead or Avonmouth.

Instead of leaping at this opportunity, the Merchant Venturers and then from 1848, the Corporation, dithered and procrastinated, and rather than lowering port dues, they increased them. By the time they came round to the idea of building a new dock, the trade and the big ships had gone elsewhere. From 1845 on, Brunel's big ships had nothing more to do with Bristol – so it is all the more ironic that the restored *Great Britain* is now a city icon. Bristol both has the boat and missed it.

There was even a poem about the city's failure to take advantage of the *Great Western*, the world's first Atlantic liner, which lost a valuable contract to carry all the transatlantic mail because of the failure to modernise the port:

> The Western an unnatural parent has,
> For all her beauty,
> Her mother never harboured her, and yet
> She asks for duty.
> Hull, Liverpool and other ports aloud
> Cry 'Go ahead!'
> A certain place that I know seems to say
> 'Reverse' instead.

Details of the Brunel story do not need re-telling here – the reckless engineer has become one of Bristol's biggest tourist assets. (See *Brunel's Bristol*, republished by Redcliffe Press in October 2005.) And although Brunel in his lifetime was a national hero, he was not entirely considered one in Bristol. This was what historian Latimer called him: 'An inexperienced theorist enamoured of novelty, prone to seek for difficulties rather than to evade them, and utterly indifferent as to the outlay which his recklessness entailed upon his employers.'

The directors of the Great Western Railway had similar problems with Brunel; he consistently went over budget and his stubborness over broad gauge, and the belief that railway companies should not share lines, had long-term financial consequences – in the end it cost £1,000,000 to change GWR and Bristol and Gloucester lines over to narrow gauge.

On the subject of broad gauge, Latimer again struck hard, calling it 'a deplorable error of the original board in neglecting the sober-minded, practical and economical engineers of the North,' and wrote of the evil commercial consequences of Brunel's 'pet crochet', which left the West of England cut-off tradewise, as the freight went on to narrow gauge lines elsewhere. The last broad gauge lines were taken up as late as 1892.

Then there was the over-spend. The original GWR share capital was fixed on Brunel's advice at £2,500,000, but before the line to London was completed, the directors had to ask for votes to bring expenditure up to £6,300,000, and this did not include the cost of building Paddington station. By 1844, the cost had risen to £8,160,000.

And Brunel was not easy to work with. He was an inspired visionary and a tireless worker himself, but he was also an impatient autocrat who supervised everything personally, issuing a stream of orders, and he found it hard to delegate, trusting no-one to do the job properly, and complaining 'I am obliged to do all myself'. He wrote scorching letters to

Brunel's Temple Meads railway station. The fares on the side of the horse-drawn carriages say Clifton six pence, Hotwells three pence (pronounced thruppence).

employees who were inefficient. In 1843 he sent this one: 'You are an accursed, lazy, inattentive, apathetic vagabond and if you continue to neglect my instructions and to show such infernal laziness, I shall send you about your business.'

When the GWR was completed, Bristolians found that train travel, except in the first class, was not very comfortable: there was no heating, and no lighting in the carriages; those who wanted to read brought their own patent candle-holders. The trains were a hunting ground for pickpockets and handbag snatchers, and there were familiar problems with graffiti, vandalism, obstacles placed on the line, and things thrown from bridges. Women were sometimes attacked in closed carriages.

Nor were Bristolians always grateful. When the Suspension Bridge (another city icon) finally was finished and opened in 1864, to national and local acclaim, exclusive Clifton, rather than welcoming an important new link with north Somerset, complained that the bridge would attract trippers and sightseers, and encourage more building on the Leigh Woods side. The bridge also attracted suicides: 'It seems to me that every person within the sight of it finds the first thought a melancholy one and the talk of every visitor is suicide,' wrote a reader of the *Clifton Chronicle*.

The spin-off Brunel created through his projects wasn't fully appreciated at the time; he created hundreds of new jobs, boosted shipbuilding in the city docks, generated the new industries of locomotive and wagon building, as well as providing endless work for the ironfounders. He also built Bristol a new hotel, the Royal Western Hotel, which opened in 1839, and is now council offices. The idea was that passengers who had travelled on the GWR would spend the night there before embarking on the *Great Western* for the voyage to New York.

While Brunel had made leaving the city easier, there was still the problem of getting around inside the city. The Corporation licensed and laid down set fares for the cabs – short for cabriolet, a two-wheeled one-horse chaise with a large hood – which could be hired at one of the 15 licensed cab stands around the city.

Later came the improved hansom cab (named after the designer, brother of Charles, architect of Clifton College) which held two people and was driven from a dickey behind; the fly, a one-horse covered carriage which was driven by the hirer; and the growler, a two-wheeled cab introduced in 1865. From 1860, bicycles gradually became an alternative, as roads improved thanks to macadamization, the invention of Bristol's first general surveyor of roads, John McAdam. By 1900, 30 miles of Bristol's roads had got the treatment.

After the 1850s, the city council began to take responsibility for lighting, refuse collection, sweeping and watering roads, and from 1845 embarked on a series of road improvements, widening the main arteries and creating new streets, both in the centre of the city, and in the ever-growing suburbs. Life for pedestrians and horse-drawn traffic became easier.

But the suburban train network took a long time to materialise: the only GWR station was at Keynsham, until St Anne's opened in 1898. The first suburban station was opened at Bedminster in 1854, followed by Fishponds in 1866, while the opening of the line to South Wales brought stations at Lawrence Hill and Stapleton Road. The Clifton Down line did not open to passengers until 1885, and the network did not cover the entire city until the turn of the century.

By that time there was an alternative public transport system – the 'street railway' or tram. The city wanted to run its own service, and the idea had been discussed as early as

Bristol's first horse tram service, seen here at the top of Maudlin Street in 1875. [from *The People's Carriage*, 1974]

The Clifton Rocks Railway in the 1890s.

1865, but private enterprise won; the man behind the launching of the Bristol Tramways Company was George White, a typical example of a lower-class boy making good. He went on to have fingers in several pies and got the nickname the Napoleon of Bristol.

The first horse-drawn tram ran from Perry Road to Blackboy on August 9, 1875, through streets decked with bunting and the Mayor who travelled in the first car said that 'every man, woman and child would be glad to save their legs'. Cheering thousands watched the new tramcars with their scarlet and white livery ascend the hill up to Clifton, church bells were rung and when the service opened to the public, some travellers were so impressed that they stayed on all afternoon. 'They was no sooner up than they was back,' said one fan, sampling the 30-minute return journey which cost 2d.

The tramcars which seated 32 on two decks were luxurious, with velvet cushions downstairs and gilt-framed landscapes on the wall, and sliding doors to the platforms at either end. Tram travel was so popular that it expanded rapidly to cover most of the city, the only competition being the horse-drawn omnibus. The first electric tram, from Old Market to Kingswood, ran in 1895, and George White told his guests at the Grand Hotel that 'Bristolians have before them one of the most convincing proofs of the marvellous process of scientific evolution through which they are passing.' The whole system was electrified by 1900.

The arrival of the tramway system shaped modern Bristol, for it meant decentralisation. The suburbs could expand because people could now travel to work, school, church, park

The present Temple Meads railway station under construction in 1876. [Colin Maggs Collection]
Hotwells: railway staff in the 1890s in front of an Avonmouth-bound train. [M.J. Tozer Collection]

An unflustered Miss Hughes poses at the National Telephone Exchange in High Street. It opened with just 32 subscribers but, by 1894 when this photograph was taken, it could accommodate 1200.
[Reece Winstone Archive]

or theatre; this in turn had an effect on shopping, with the opening of more suburban shopping parades and less reliance on markets in the city centre. Manufacturing firms could re-locate, the de-industrialisation of the central area slowly started, and the service industries could move in. New buildings in the centre of the city now tended to be offices, not manufactories.

The popularity of bicycles, from the 1870s on, also had an impact. Workers could now cycle to work and to the shops, and make outings into Somerset, so much so that the Suspension Bridge officials had a rule that 'bicycles and velocipedes should not be ridden over the bridge, as it makes the horses shy'.

One more short-lived means of transport was the Clifton Rocks Railway, built by publisher Sir George Newnes from Hotwells up through a tunnel in the rock to his hotel, the Grand Spa, in Clifton. It was a 240ft. hydraulic railway, 2d. up 1d. down, and designed to bring up tourists arriving by steamer at the Hotwell Wharf, servants who worked up in Clifton, and tram-users who had to go that way round because Clifton refused to have trams any nearer to the village than Queen's Road. It ran from 1893 until 1934. The public was reassured that 'the cars cannot run down the incline by themselves, and if left untouched even after they have started on their journey, they will stop perfectly still gripping the rails with a tremendous vice-like tenacity.' The railway is now being partially restored.

Telegraphic communication had arrived in 1852, but the telephone service came much later, in 1879, when the Exchange in the High Street opened with just 32 subscribers. The service, covering the city only, cost £18 a year if you lived over half a mile from the exchange and £14. 10s, if under. At first private sub-scribers were few and largely lived in Clifton, but businesses began to realise how this new invention could speed up trade if they could order and take orders by phone.

What the smart postman wore in mid-century. [Post Office Copyright Reserved]

But when Queen Victoria died in 1901, tele-phone subscribers were a tiny minority in the city; the rest of the population relied on an extremely efficient postal service. Before the Penny Post Act of 1839, the Post Office in Exchange Avenue had only six clerks as indoor staff, and sending a letter was an expensive luxury. The Post Office in Bristol expanded with increased literacy; in 1859, there were only three branches, one of them being in Clifton, and only 15 pillar boxes throughout the city. By 1901, there were 76 Post Offices and 186 letter boxes, with over 70 million letters being delivered annually. Letters were collected 12 times a day, and delivered six times a day. You could write a letter in the morning, post it, and get a reply by the afternoon. It's one area where, until the coming of email, the Victorians won hands down over the twenty-first century.

Snapshots of Communications

Advertisement for the first sailings of the *Great Western*, March 1838
There are 128 state rooms divided between the upper saloon, under saloon, forecabin, poop, and cuddy, all of one class, with a fare of 35 guineas. There are also 20 good bed places for servants who travel at half fare, as also do children and there is stowage for a small quantity of light goods at a % per ton.

The first class dining salon is really a beautiful room. Down the centre are 12 principal columns of white and gold with ornamental capitals. Twelve similar columns also range down the walls on either side. The archways of several doors are tastefully covered and gilded, and are surmounted with neat medallioned heads. The walls are of a delicate lemon-tinted drab hue, relieved with blue white and gold.

A typical menu offered a choice of 27 first courses, nine second and six desserts, after starting with soup.

Launch of the *Great Britain*

From the water's edge upwards rose tier upon tier of spectators, some arranged in gardens, some perched in scaffolding, some stationed at windows, and upon housetops, the whole presenting a beautifully diversified and broken picture of irregular rising ground crowded with people and wavered over all by gay flags. There could not be less than 30,000 people on Brandon Hill. A shower of rain came on at about two o'clock and the appearance of the hill was then curious in the extreme, as if by word of command with almost military precision, as nearly every individual on the hill spread an umbrella. It looked like one large variegated tent – blue, green, brown – of every variety of shade in silk and cotton. After the launch there was a banquet on board for 600 people.
Felix Farley's Journal, July 1843

A schoolboy watches Prince Albert arrive at the station

He is a very handsome young man though he looked rather pale and tired. There was very little cheering I thought, though in the newspapers of course it said that he was received with loud and continued acclamation of the multitude. His route lay through the most fashionable parts of Clifton; there were triumphal arches and a handsome Pavilion, erected in a yard by the vessel, was covered in flags of all description.

By Mr Cross's influence we got admission to a range of seats placed just outside Clifton National School Room, where there was a nice view of the vessel … the papers say she was christened by the Prince hurling a bottle of Champagne at her but in reality Mrs. Miles tried to perform the operation and being clumsy or nervous, instead of throwing the bottle let it drop out of her hand into the water, so the vessel was not christened at all, perhaps it is a bad omen. She is now to be seen at a shilling a head.
Letter from William Prideaux, 1843

Prince Albert travels on the GWR

The greatest speed which I have personally witnessed occurred on the return of a train from Bristol, on the occasion of the floating of the *Great Britain*. I was in a compartment, in conversation with three eminent engineers, when one of them remarked the unusual speed of the train: my neighbour on my left took out his watch, and noted the time of passage of the distance posts, when it appeared that we were then travelling at the rate of 78 miles an hour. The train was on an incline and we did not long sustain that dangerous velocity.
Prince Albert

Sailing on the *Great Britain*

The *Great Britain* sailed at 3 amidst a triumphant salute from her own guns (she carried two cannons). The whole line of the docks was crowded with people watching and cheering and many steamers (full from end to end) accompanied us down the river. We

Welsh Back quayside.

had dinner at 4, it was very calm none of the passengers were ill, so we had the opportunity of seeing each other's faces. There are a little more than 80 in the After Saloon, and half as many again in the Fore Saloon. [After was first class, and a ticket to Australia cost 70 guineas. Fore was second class.] About 20 sat at each table, we are at the Captain's. I did not go up on deck after dinner, and to bed soon after, where I slept soundly, notwithstanding the small cabin.

Ann Henning's Journal

Valedictory tribute to Brunel by Daniel Gooch, 1859

By his death the greatest of England's engineers was lost, the man with the greatest originality of thought and power of execution, bold in his plans but right. The commercial world thought him extravagant; but although he was so, great things are not done by those who sit down and count the cost of every thought and act.

Rail travel, 1851

On entering the yard, you find, amidst the greatest apparent confusion, the most perfect order. A porter is ready to conduct you to the booking office, where you pay your fare and receive a ticket; you then ascend a flight of stairs to the platform. Having taken your place, and made all ready, you are now at ease to observe what is going on, if time permits. The scene is truly interesting. Numbers of persons are at the Station, all engaged as yourself, either in doing or seeing what is done. Meanwhile passengers increase with equal bustle, and you are then amused by the conductor responding to various questions: 'London, Ma'am? In this carriage. Reading Sir? In that.'

You now look round and see several engines with red hot fires in their bodies, and volumes of condensed steam issuing from them; one of them moves slowly towards you. The huge piece bellows at first like an elephant: deep, slow, and terrific are the hoarse heavings that it makes. It is then linked to the carriages. The conductor has done his part

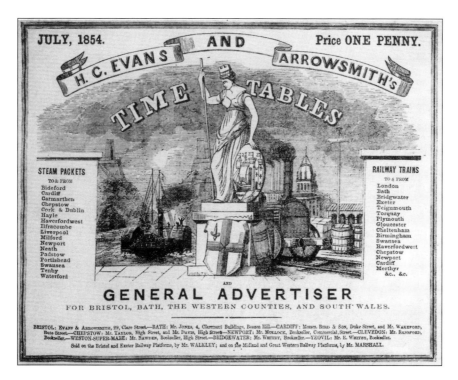

JULY, 1854.   AND   Price ONE PENNY.

H. C. EVANS   ARROWSMITH'S

TIME TABLES

STEAM PACKETS
TO & FROM
Bideford
Cardiff
Carmarthen
Chepstow
Cork & Dublin
Hayle
Haverfordwest
Ilfracombe
Liverpool
Milford
Newport
Neath
Padstow
Portishead
Swansea
Tenby
Waterford

RAILWAY TRAINS
TO & FROM
London
Bath
Bridgwater
Exeter
Teignmouth
Torquay
Plymouth
Gloucester
Cheltenham
Birmingham
Swansea
Haverfordwest
Chepstow
Newport
Cardiff
Merthyr
&c., &c.

AND

GENERAL ADVERTISER
FOR BRISTOL, BATH, THE WESTERN COUNTIES, AND SOUTH WALES.

BRISTOL: EVANS & ARROWSMITH, 29, Clare Street—BATH: Mr. JONES, 4, Claremont Buildings, Beacon Hill—CARDIFF: Messrs. BIRD & SON, Duke Street, and Mr. WAKEFORD, Bute Street—CHEPSTOW: Mr. TAYLOR, High Street, and Mr. DAVIS, High Street—NEWPORT: Mr. MULLOCK, Bookseller, Commercial Street—CLEVEDON: Mr. RANSFORD, Bookseller.—WESTON-SUPER-MARE: Mr. BAWDEN, Bookseller, High Street—BRIDGWATER: Mr. WHITBY, Bookseller, High Street.—YEOVIL: Mr. E. WHITBY, Bookseller.
Sold on the Bristol and Exeter Railway Platforms, by Mr. WALKLEY; and on the Midland and Great Western Railway Platforms, by Mr. MARSHALL.

and is seated; the guard is inside his box at the back of the first carriage; a whistle is sounded as a signal for starting – and you are off.

Morgan's New Guide to Bristol, 1851

Heating in trains, 1895

We are glad to observe that the question of the adoption of improved methods for heating their carriages, [is being addressed] and that the GWR company are fully alive to the necessity for superseding the antiquated cumbrous hot water tins commonly known as footwarmers.

Bristol Mercury editorial

Rules for Hackney Coaches and Cars, 1851

When there are Four Persons inside and One outside a Coach, or Three Persons inside and One outside a Chariot, or Three persons inside or Two persons inside, and One outside a Fly, the Driver shall not be obliged to take any Luggage, except Carpet bags, Parcels, or Packages, to be carried in the hand or between the feet of the passengers; but the person hiring the Carriage shall be allowed to have a reasonable quantity of Luggage, not exceeding Eighty-four pounds in weight for each person short of the number above mentioned.

The Bristol hansom cab

They are the most uncomfortable that I have ever sat and chafed in. The body is thrown back at an angle of some 15 degrees, which is acute in its painfulness, and makes the

The Yatton Carrier, J.E.White. [*Country Carriers in the Bristol Region in the late Nineteenth Century*, Kenneth Morgan, Bristol Branch of the Historical Association. Photograph kindly supplied by Mrs Sylvia Starr]

parting with it and the half crown (which appears to be the minimum fare in this wealthy old city) a thing of gladness.

Lesser Columbus, 1893

State of the roads

It is discreditable that a main road leading from Regent Street to Prince's Buildings should be allowed to remain in the condition it is and has been for years. From Messrs. Lewis to the end are a series of stables with coach houses having double doors opening outwards. Consequently it frequently happens that a passer-by gets knocked down. The next evil is the ostler who, indifferent as to the comfort of passers-by, keeps the doors open across the pavement while he washes the carriage between them; passengers have to take to the road whatever condition it may be in. Another abominable nuisance is that the dung or manure pits are in the pavement.

Letter to Clifton Chronicle, 1886

Work on the Suspension Bridge, 1863

The work seems to go on in perfect silence for at the distance at which we stand it is impossible to catch the slightest sound either of voice or implement. The workers suspended in mid-air are to our view scarcely so large as spiders and like spiders the busy hands and feet seem to crouch and cluster on a web airy and light as gossamer. One wonders how the men can maintain their position on a structure of apparent thread and still more how they can retain their self-possession and working faculties while balanced at the height of some 300 feet above the water.

The opening of the Suspension Bridge

Band after band poured forth their joyous strains, salvoes of artillery were being discharged and all nature seemed animated and vocal with rejoicing… A crowd of 100,000 gathered to see the first triumphal crossing led by contractors Cochrane and Grove, and his workmen, followed by consuls, clergy, county dignitaries, directors, the Mayor and civic party, to a salute of guns. The explorer Dr. Livingstone was one of the first members of the public to walk across.

Clifton Chronicle, December, 1864

Suicide from the Suspension Bridge

Mr George Wellington Green, 52, family man, whose brothers were an Alderman and a shipowner, lived at Portishead. He presented himself at the tollhouse and appeared to be in thoughtful mood and was observed to press his hand to his head as if suffering from some painful sensation there … Almost immediately afterwards, he placed his hand upon the railings of the bridge, which are about 4ft high, and jumped over. His body was observed to twirl over as it descended and then fall with a heavy thud upon the mud of the Avon, where the tide had receded. Notwithstanding the terrific height of the fall, about 280 feet, no bones were broken and with the exception of some bruises on the temple, the body was not at all disfigured.

Clifton Chronicle, May 1866

Elsie and Ruby Brown survive being thrown over the Suspension Bridge by their father in 1896.

[The wind and high tide saved them, for they landed just a few feet from a pilot boat.] It was dark and raining and father carried little sister Elsie. Father paid a penny each for us to go on the bridge and said he was looking for the nearest way to the station. We stayed in the bridge about an hour. I was soaking wet and so was Elsie. Father caught hold of me and I began to scream. He lifted me up on the side of the Bridge and put me over, I clung on to him, he loosened my hands and I fell.

Ruby Brown's Memoirs

Plus ça change

It is a grave error to rush through life, I think, and so evidently does the Bristol Tramways. You may have to wait a quarter of an hour at any particular terminus of this particular tramways system. Now I am safe in asserting that no other business community in the kingdom would be satisfied with such an audaciously infrequent service as this. The tramcar conductors are dirty, rude, disobliging and objectionable. He has never been known to disqualify himself for the position he holds by saying 'Thank you' or by answering a tremblingly uttered request for information civilly.

Lesser Columbus, 1893

Clifton objects to a Sunday omnibus service

May I through your columns make a most decided and earnest protest against the commencement of Sunday omnibus traffic in this part of Clifton. Clifton has long been famed for its quiet and orderly Sunday. Have the directors no consideration for their horses or their men?

... and to an extension of the electric tram service

Electric cars would bring people to Clifton perhaps, but what sort of people. Penny trampers are no use to Clifton, they will not fill our empty houses. By all means let them enjoy the pleasures of the Downs in common with ourselves, no-one would wish to deny them that.

Let us try all we can to raise the tone of Clifton, not lower it. We want carriages here, not noisy electric cars. If I were to learn that the trams were presently to pass my door, I would sell my house with the least possible delay.

Letters to Clifton Chronicle

Clifton Rocks Railway opens, March 1893

The opening took Clifton by surprise – only a dozen or so were present at the time arranged for starting the first car, 9am. There are four sets of rails, two for going up, two for going down and the motive power is supplied by an ingenious arrangement. Each car can balance the other and to overcome weight variations, water is pumped in or out of a large tank underneath each car. There were a few slight hitches: two faulty awkward stops at the top and doors opening outwards instead of sliding. The cars themselves are comfortable and airy, each seating 18 persons and lit by oil lamps, but the tunnel is so steep that daylight can only penetrate from top to bottom. We believe it is the intention to have electric light installed.

Over 6,000 persons used the lift on the first day and a large number of those travelling early and paying double the fare were able to secure a pleasing little memento of the occasion, a gilded Maltese cross.

Clifton Chronicle

Middle-class gentility: tea on the lawn at Rupert House, St Michael's Hill, 1860s.
[Reece Winstone Archive]

7 – Home sweet home

THOUSANDS OF MODERN BRISTOLIANS LIVE IN VICTORIAN HOUSES. But their lives are very different: when these terraces and villas were built in the boom from the 1860s onwards, they would have been mainly for rent. They would have been lit by oil lamps, or later gas, they had coal fires, earth-closets and rarely a fitted bathroom.

Speculators and builders put them up, and often sold them on unfurnished; a small terraced house cost around £100 to build and would have been rented at £30 a year, so a clerk earning £100 a year could just afford one. If he sold, the builder expected to make 10 per cent on his costs. A really grand semi-detached mansion in Clifton could cost up to £2,500 to build. Those who did purchase rather than rent could get a mortgage from Bristol and West Building Society, founded in 1850. By the 1880s there were over 20 building societies in the city, but until the turn of the century, 90 per cent of homes were still rented.

These were mass-produced houses built in runs of ten to twenty at a time, on a standard pattern, either semi-detached, or terraced. The semi-detached villa had a drawing room, dining room and breakfast room on the ground floor, and in the case of the terrace, a parlour in the front, breakfast room at the back; upstairs would be family bedrooms, a nursery, and maybe a dressing room and an earth-closet. Water would be heated on the range in the basement. The cheapest homes were on two floors with a kitchen extension at the rear.

Thanks to their uniformity, the components could now be mass produced. Woodworking machinery introduced in the 1840s meant doors and windows could be standardised, steam saws at the quarries led to mass-produced stone lintels, sills and door frames, all of which could now be transported by rail. The housing boom led to growth in all the ancillary trades, glazing, plumbing, plastering, paint manufacture, gas fitting, joinery, and meant more work for local estate agents, auctioneers, surveyors and solicitors.

The standard of building also improved following a series of planning acts which dictated the inclusion of a damp course, and adequate light and ventilation, rules about the distance between houses, the need for an open area at the back, and the width of the road, which accounts for the conformity in Victorian streets wherever you go. The scale of the building was breathtaking: nationally, six million new homes were built between 1801 and 1901, and two million of these were erected between 1870 and 1901.

A handful of the firms which built and fitted these Bristol houses are still trading: builders Cowlins, John Perkins, Stone, Cattybrook for bricks, Mogfords for decorating,

Plasterers enjoying a Victorian building boom. [Bristol Museums and Art Gallery]

Robbins timber, Purimachos who supplied fireproof cement, Bell for stained glass, Farvis for conservatory ironwork, Sturge for a survey, Garaways for gardening supplies, and house-hunters might have gone to Hole, the estate agent, and organised their removal with Pickfords.

For this was the age of the home of your own. The newly created middle classes now wanted somewhere different to live. Until around 1840, unless you were very rich, you expected to live in a terrace, but the newly wealthy rebelled. They wanted a home that was more distinctive, something with a bit of ornament, bay windows, a decorative roofline, and as the century proceeded, facades grew more and more decorative. The flat-faced Georgian stucco and stone and brick was out of date, and the textured local pink rubble stone, or sandstone and ashlar, was the new fashion.

The housing legacy of the Victorians is visible everywhere in the city but what we lost in the process were many fine Tudor and Jacobean big houses which the Victorians regarded as old-fashioned and insanitary – they wanted iron and stone to replace lath and plaster. The Victorians were keen demolishers, and there was no need for a planning application. All over the heart of the city, hundreds of the jetted and gabled timber-frame houses and shops were destroyed, and the rubble buried in the cellars below, thus also destroying a unique part of underground Bristol.

The greatest losses were Sir John Young's Great House, the Elizabethan mansion which stood where the Colston Hall is today, demolished in 1863, and Canynges's fifteenth-century mansion in Redcliffe Street, lost in the 1880s in the name of progress.

Sedate Sion Hill when Clifton not only thought itself, but actually was, a different world from the smoky industrial city.

(Bristol's Victorian domestic architecture may not be particularly distinguished but the public, commercial and industrial buildings are outstanding: national critics of the day praised Bristol's Byzantine warehouses, grand banks, elegant churches and handsome public buildings, like the Guildhall in Broad Street, the Grand Hotel, the Victoria Rooms, the RWA and Clifton College.)

The average private homes were less grand, but aspiring, decorated inside in dark colours, brown or green, and if there was any wallpaper (from Cotterells) it would be dark too. Floors were stained wood, or covered with the forerunner to linoleum, a printed or painted oilcloth floor covering made by the famous Bristol manufacturer, Hare's, who could do you a copy of a Roman pavement. Furniture, dark-stained oak or mahogany, might come from Maggs in Queen's Road, or from the higher-class Trapnell and Gane in College Green, and the rich would order from Laverton's, who provided the furnishings at Tyntesfield. Most homes would have a piano, purchased at Duck Son and Pinker, or from Dimoline of Denmark Street, who had shown a papier mâché model at the Great Exhibition.

In a reaction against Georgian plainness, the Victorian house would be filled with knick-knacks, displayed on whatnots, and plants (from Garaways in Whiteladies Road), mainly aspidistras because they were the only plants which could survive the leaky gas lighting, and objects under glass domes. Prints and reproductions of paintings (from Frost and Reed) often religious, would crowd the walls, and china would be on display everywhere. For this was the first age of the consumer. The Industrial Revolution

The dining room at 24 College Road, Clifton in 1893.

bought salaries that allowed employees some disposable income, and a myriad of goods were being made to help them spend it, hence the popularity in Bristol of bazaar-style shopping. But while the homes of the middle class were crammed with objects, the homes of the poor were bare.

For class, as in all aspects of life in Victorian Bristol, was evident in the choice of house and where it was. The poor lived in atrocious unhealthy old houses, in the central areas of Bristol. The industrial and factory workers lived near work in cheap terraced housing, often built by their employers; between them the Smythes, who owned the collieries, and Wills, changed the face of Bedminster and Southville this way. The same happened in Barton Hill thanks to the Great Western cotton factory.

(Meanwhile the Smythes at Ashton Court had 13,000 acres, an income in 1872 of £44,360 a year, and were the third richest family in Somerset, with 20 per cent of their wealth coming from collieries, the rest from land. In 1884 they even had a visit from Royalty, when the Prince of Wales went shooting on the estate.)

The lower-middle class, the tradespeople and clerks, were now wealthy enough to move out to the suburbs, away from the noise and pollution, to Horfield or St Andrews,

Fishponds, Henleaze or Bishopston and buy or rent more substantial homes, semi-detached or terraced. The upper-middle classes, the business and professionals, aspired to a fully-fledged villa, with a shrubbery, garden, tennis court and conservatory, in Redland or Clifton, where these large families lived in some style, with several servants, a governess and coachman. Home life was very important to the Victorians, thanks to the example set by Queen Victoria herself. The Georgian terraces did not announce status – the new Victorian villas did.

The new middle class also had to adapt to the lifestyle, especially the women who had to learn to become ladies: they needed to know how to manage servants, how to budget and shop, how to socialise, how to entertain, and they turned to magazines and books, and blessed Mrs Beeton and her book of *Everyday Cookery and Housekeeping*, published in 1865.

While the men carried on their occupations, away from home, women had to learn how to be the mistress of a household in which she supervised, rather than worked herself. Being the mistress of a household became a career in itself, for in a respectable middle-class family the idea of wives and daughters working was out of the question.

The mistress did not have to shop, except for her private needs, for she would send a servant to fetch what she had ordered; she only had to know what to buy and where to buy it. She did not have to cook, but she had to know about recipes and menus, she did not have to lay tables or wash up but she had to know how to instruct her servants to do it properly. She would not do the cleaning herself, but she had to know the theory to instruct the servants. Victorian homes were highly labour-intensive, what with the daily polishing, dusting and step whitening and laundry, boot-cleaning, scrubbing and ironing.

This is how Mrs Beeton saw the typical day of a middle-class wife who has risen at seven to supervise breakfast and order the day's meals:

> The following work a mistress should do. Two hours devoted to the house and morning duties brings one to eleven o'clock; on Monday the mending must be carefully executed up to lunchtime. A daily walk should be taken, weather permitting, and the lady should first go and order anything required for the house, then return visits, or take a good constitutional until four o'clock. From four to five, write letters or read for an hour (serious reading, leaving light reading for evening).

> At five, when necessary, go downstairs to speak to the cook. Glance round to see all preparations are getting forward for the six o'clock dinner; then go upstairs, inspect the housemaid's performance of needlework, always laid in your room for that purpose, and dress for dinner. Go into the dining room and see all is ready, put out the wine, arrange dessert and flowers. Then be ready at a quarter to six to receive le mari, and see that he has his hot water, slippers, etc. At six, dinner, after which coffee and amusements of music, reading, cards or needlework of a light nature.

That was just Monday; Tuesday Thursday and Friday could be devoted to the garden and plants, the afternoons to walking or driving, and hobbies or study.

One of the great problems for middle-class Victorian women was filling up leisure time in a socially acceptable way. It was fortunate that they had so much leisure, for it meant they were free to do charity work, and a permanent occupation for ladies was preparation for the annual church bazaar; they knitted, sewed, painted furniture, made doileys, framed pictures in passé-partout, made screens, fans, hair-tidies, sweets and cakes, they collected bric-a-brac and white elephants, and sold all these things to the public, mainly ladies like themselves, to raise money for a mission or a church charity.

Visiting the poor of the parish was another suitable occupation, but they had to be respectable, grateful poor. They would take soup, and cast-off clothes and read to them, but they had to do it sensitively, as *The Girl's Own Paper* of 1880 reminded:

> It is no unusual thing to find the lady district visitor think she may leave all her lady's manners behind her in the drawing room when she goes out to pay her daily calls to the cottages of her poorer neighbours. There is no greater mistake than this in the whole sphere of parish work.

> Therefore when a woman of position and education far above their own enters their houses pouring forth questions full of noisy curiosity, or sits by their fireside criticising freely their dress or furniture or rooms, unasked all over their dwellings, prescribing all sorts of improvements and changes, they naturally enough either grow rude and impertinent, or else shrink into a shell of timid, injured silence.

Another major time-filler was visiting other ladies, following the rituals of dressing up, leaving cards, taking tea and having conversations; in the evening there were soirées, with music and recitations and displays of amateur artwork. Only late in the century did the fetters of home loosen somewhat, when it became acceptable for women to play tennis, sing in a choir, ride a bicycle, join a class of study.

For the children of a Victorian household in Bristol, life was fun. They had toys bought for them at La Trobe's Toy Bazaar, they went skating, boating, they had improving literature (including the historical novels by Bristol's own Emma Marshall) bought for them from George's in Park Street, there were theatricals on the Downs, funfairs at the Zoo. They were allowed a certain amount of freedom, as they got older, as Francis Newbolt the Clifton College schoolboy, reveals in his diary account of his summer vacation in 1870s Clifton:

> We lay in hammocks, ate ices at Pomeroys, played cricket on the Downs, took bicycle rides, played fives, and card games, went to the baths, did chemical experiments, visited the Zoo and the dentist.

The men of the household had never had it so good. Their word was law, they were revered as the head of the household, waited on hand and foot, free to go off to eat out

Domestic bliss: the scene in almost any Clifton drawing room towards the end of Victoria's reign.

(respectable ladies didn't), go to a music hall (ditto) and to the club or the pub, or possibly, the brothel. Prince Albert set the fashion for the manly pater familias, and their new homes were designed to show off this status.

They were also houses expressly designed for servants to work in, with a kitchen in the basement, and rooms in the attic for servants to sleep in. Even a clerk like Mr Pooter (in *Diary of a Nobody*) on £150–£200 a year could afford to pay £5 a year for a live-in maid-of-all-work. The mid-century rule was roughly that earnings of £250–£300 warranted one maidservant, £450 to £500 warranted a cook and a housemaid, £500 to £700, a cook, a housemaid and a bootboy. For wages were low: a cook earned £20 a year, a parlourmaid £16, a housemaid £12, and a kitchen maid £6. With no official school leaving age, children could start work as a servant at the age of 10 or 12.

If the daily routine was demanding for the mistress of the house, it was virtual slavery for the servants who effectively worked from six am to midnight, with one half day off a week, for pitiful wages. In 1851, of the eight million females over ten years old, one million were in service. For the rural poor who had come to Bristol for work, becoming a servant was almost inevitable – and raw country girls were especially prized, as an advertisement in the *Bristol Times* for 1888 shows: 'Kitchen Maid wanted on a schoolhouse, from country preferred; must be strong, good scrubber and thoroughly respectable.'

Then there were Bristol institutions that educated poor children to become servants; until educational reforms, all Bristol's charity schools, orphanages, reformatories and workhouses provided a useful supply of servants for the middle classes. They kitted them out with work clothing when they left, and young boys or girls leaving the workhouse had to be found jobs that paid 'not less than one shilling a week'.

Living in was an extra burden for a servant, for they got cast off furniture and bedding, no fires, no comforts – employers didn't want them spoiled, and many thought they should be treated like children, a race apart. One Clifton wife got a very rare and shameful divorce from her army captain husband on the grounds of 'intimacy with a servant'.

Some upper servants did get the chance to live out, at the Domestic Servants' Institution in Dover Place, Clifton, which in 1875 'furnishes at moderate charges lodgings for female servants of good character who must bring with them a satisfactory reference'.

For servants the reference or 'character' was all important – in the *Western Daily Press* a servant girl advertised for her lost character, and this didn't mean she had fallen into sin but that she had lost the piece of paper with her last employer's all-important reference on it.

Right up to the death of the Queen there were still ample supplies of servants to work in Bristol's thousands of new villas and terraces, but things were changing. Better education meant that the servant class had a greater choice of occupation, and some of them, fired by the example of the middle classes, actually aspired to a home of their own. It was every Victorian Bristolian's dream.

Snapshots of Home

New Redland villa to let, 1852
To be let, a newly built villa in Redland with noble dining room and drawing rooms, breakfast room, seven bedrooms, two capital and convenient kitchens, two water closets, soft and spring water, two good cellars, back and front gardens with choice trees, stable for two or three horses with coachhouse and sleeping apartment for servant over. The drainage is excellent, the neighbourhood highly respectable, the air is salubrious and the views extensive and picturesque.

Modern improvements
The interesting and very picturesque houses in this city are so rapidly disappearing altogether, or yielding to modern improvements, that our readers will be glad to know where those best worthy of inspection may be still seen. While we are writing the Bush Tavern opposite the exchange is hourly disappearing and in a few days nothing will be left of that well-known house.
Curiosities of Bristol, 1853

Building mania
Many living have made hay (literally) in The Mall and Caledonia Place, and not long

since in Clifton Park. The little farmhouse where they sell fresh butter, near Litfield Place, will soon be shut out of sight by a cordon of domestic palaces. It seems but as yesterday that the Victoria Rooms and another building were the only edifices in that direction north of Berkeley Square.

Bristol Times, 1855

Jerry building

New buildings are being carried up in Clifton with marvellous rapidity, in some cases indeed with so much rapidity that they do not get strengthened enough in their progress to remain up. Walkers in Clyde Road, Westcott Park, on the first of this month saw a pair of what are called semi-detached villas, partly roofed, with bow windows and everything pretty but when they passed next morning, they found in their place only a heap of dusty rubbish … the workmanship was very bad.

The Builder, 1868

A handsome detached residence

To let: Upper Belgrave Road, close to College and schools, overlooking Durdham and Clifton Downs, to let furnished, handsome detached residence standing in its own grounds. It is fully and handsomely furnished and decorated and contains on the ground floor a fine entrance hall, dining room, drawing room, music room or study, wc, lavatory, pantries. On the first floor three fine bedrooms, dressing room and fitted bathroom (hot and cold) housemaid's closet and wc. On the second floor, four bedrooms, dressing room, tower staircase leading to fine look-out. The basement offices are exceptionally spacious and convenient. To be let at the exceedingly low rent of five guineas a week, and a family with careful children would be no objection.

Bristol Times, 1880

Rats!

Eighteen years ago I bought an excellent large house – the vendor was the builder, the house was a new one and superb in all respects but one. Drains. My neighbour and I were pestered with drain rats and they and their servants ailed with sudden symptoms. Repairs to drains revealed the whole system has been formed and laid in clay and were open and leaking into the basement. No cement had been used!

Clifton Chronicle, 1884

Safe wallpaper

Cotterells wallpapers of Wine Street exhibited patent engraved paper hangings printed from engraved copper rollers, the minute details of which are such as require a magnifying glass to discover their accuracy. One of them is a beautiful green which we observe bears Dr Lethaby's certification of its perfectly innocuous colour, so that it is yet possible to paper our bedrooms without the dreaded effects of arseniate of copper, of which so much has been said.

Bristol Daily Post, 1865

How the other half lived

The district of St Jude's with its thickly clustering old houses, its dark entries and back-yard shed dwellings, long enjoyed an unenviable reputation as the abode of the utmost squalor and misery, abject poverty, personal improvidence and social wrong. We have visited homes which were described to us as shed-dwellings, old sheds and outbuildings plastered over and other one-roomed hovels dark and grimy with filth, with humid floors and clammy walls, no better than cells above ground.

Homes of The Bristol Poor

Estate Agents Condemned

There are half a dozen agents' billboards in front of each deserted mansion. Can no way of checking this be devised? Could not several agents be named on one board? It gives visitors a general impression of bankruptcy.

Letter to Clifton Chronicle, 1884

Good housekeeping

If a Mistress of a household considers that she is the steward of her husband's property, and that upon her diligence, knowledge and capability depends the entire happiness of her household, she will understand how important is her post, and how any negligence on her part must necessarily repeat itself in the conduct of her domestics. It is seldom requisite that a mistress should perform other work than that of supervising her house-hold, choosing and paying for household requisites; but it is imperative that she should not be the dupe of designing servants or the ignorant director of an equally ignorant maid.

No amount of love, beauty, or of intelligence will make a home happy without a right judgment on the part of the housewife. A woman must rule her household or be ruled by it; she must hold the reins with a tight firm hand.

Isabella Beeton's Everyday Cookery and Housekeeping Book, 1865

A mistress should rise at latest at seven o'clock. This will appear dreadfully late to some notables, but will be found to be a good hour all the year round. The mistress should take her cold bath, and perform a neat careful and pretty morning toilet … she will be ready dressed to descend by eight o'clock, but before leaving her room will place two chairs at the end of the bed and turn the whole of the bedclothes over them, and except on very rainy mornings, will throw open the windows of her room … key basket in hand, she should descend to the breakfast room, at once ring for the kettle or tea urn, and make the tea, coffee, cocoa or chocolate as the case may be. Her eye should now glance over the table to see that everything required for the table is in place. As soon as the Mistress hears her husband's step, the bell should be rung for the hot dish; and should he be as business men usually are, rather pressed for time, she should herself wait upon him, cutting his bread, buttering his toast, etc. Also give standing orders that coat, hat and umbrella shall be brushed and ready; and see that they are by helping on

Game and poultry in St Nicholas Street.

the coat, handing the hat and umbrella.

Mrs Beeton

Servant etiquette

Never let your voice be heard by the ladies and gentlemen of the house except when necessary. Always stand silent and keep your hands before you, or at your sides, when you are speaking or being spoken to. For dresses, do not ever choose gay patterns or colours … they can never look becoming for servants.

The Servants' Behaviour Book, 1851

Gentleness, kindness and firmness are the qualities required in a mistress, with a thorough practical knowledge of what are her servants' duties. We may here remark that those households are best conducted where the mistress never converses with her servants; never speaks but to gently give an order, ask a question or say good morning and evening to her maids.

Mrs Beeton

Domestic service

There are many reasons for the great disinclination which girls have for domestic service … In all but large households, where there is much idleness and waste, domestic service is incessant hard work at all hours of the day and sometimes of the night too. It is at best a kind of slavery, and when a girl has a home it is only a human feeling, and one we should respect, if she prefers to undertake work in trades because she can return at night and on Sunday to the home circle.

One feasible suggestion of improvement is a system of superior charwomen under which servants could go home at night. They would then know when their work for the

"ONLY THE BEST."

GARAWAY & CO.,

FLORISTS,

WHITELADIES ROAD, CLIFTON.

SPRAYS AND OTHER FLORAL DEVICES OF CHOICEST
NATURAL FLOWERS

Carefully Packed for Parcel Post or Rail, to arrive fresh at any distance.

Choice Palms and other Foliage and Flowering Plants for House Decoration.

Loose Flowers and Ferns for the Dinner Table.

A LARGE SELECTION OF
DRIED GRASSES, PAMPAS GRASSES,
Dried Natural Flowers,
FOR CHURCH DECORATIONS, &c.

Photographic Institution, 32, Park Street.

Coloured   Photographic

PORTRAITS

(BY THE NEW PROCESS,)

ARE TAKEN FROM TEN TILL FOUR, DAILY,

AT THE

PHOTOGRAPHIC INSTITUTION,

BY

MR. VINES.

MR. VINES begs to state that no expense will be spared to render his Pictures as perfect as can be produced, and no person will be expected to take a Portrait which may be in any way unsatisfactory. The premises which he has taken are spacious and convenient, and admirably adapted for Photographic purposes. Sitters are not required to ascend higher than the drawing-room floor. The reception and exhibition rooms are especially arranged so as to ensure the comfort of visitors.

Invalids may be taken at their own Residences.

DAGUERREOTYPES AND PAINTINGS OF EVERY DESCRIPTION ACCURATELY COPIED.

A FEW NOTICES OF THE PRESS ARE APPENDED.

From the Bristol Mercury.
" Mr. Vines, of the Photographic Institution, Park-street, has succeeded in effecting an improvement in Daguerreotype Portraits which will, we think, render them quite as acceptable as the ivory miniature. The improvement consists in accelerating the process by means of electricity, and then tinting the portraits, in an agreeable and life-like manner."
From the Bristol Mirror.
" Nothing can be more successful, and such, we think, will be the decided opinion of such of our readers as will take the pains of personally inspecting the beautiful specimens taken by Mr. Vines."
From the Bristol Examiner.
" We have had the pleasure of inspecting the Photographic Institution, Park-street. The numerous specimens exhibited demonstrate the high state of perfection to which the art has been brought. Taken by the unerring process of nature from life, they must be true to life."
From the Bristol Gazette.
" The new process fully merits the extensive patronage it has received."
From the Somerset County Gazette.
" The portraits produced by Mr. Vines are some of the most perfect and beautiful we have ever seen."

day was over and their industry could be organised … heads of households might then have to wait upon themselves a little more than they do now, but much of the service now regarded as necessary is really only to gratify pride and to keep up appearances.

Emma Paterson, Bristol trade unionist, 1879

A Caution to Mistresses and Maids from the Ladies' Association for the care of Friendless Girls

We should be thankful to be allowed to point out some ways in which young servants (though possibly giddy and thoughtless) having no desire to do wrong, may be kept from falling a prey to the many agents of evil who are ever on the watch to lay a snare for their feet.

1. Danger of leaving a simple servant in charge of a house during the absence of the family.

2. We are most anxious to induce mistresses not to let young servants go out, especially in Bank Holidays, to places of amusement without enquiring the nature of the entertainment and the character of the companions who will accompany them.

3. Evil arises from mistresses allowing young servants too much liberty in the evenings or on Sundays. In some of the saddest cases the mischief has originated (from sheer ignorance of danger) by accepting the invitation of a stranger and taking a walk after Sunday evening service.

From A Lady Inviting Another To Aid A Charity

My dear Mrs …

Numbering you as I do among the philanthropic of our little world, I have no hesitation in saying your aid is required in a new channel which we are endeavouring to open up before the severity of the winter approaches its height. By we I mean a few mutual friends who, like yourself, think that the shortest route to happiness is that which brings something in the shape of comfort to those who are destitute of it and know what it means. We are striving to raise sufficient money to buy sixty loads of coal, the quantity which we think will enable our poor to keep warm for a month or two, and if the calls on your goodness are not too great already, I shall hope to say that you have joined us.

Believe me,

My dear Mrs …

Ever sincerely Yours, …

From Mrs Beeton's Complete Letter-Writer

Amelia Edwards, the Egyptologist, describes her Westbury-on-Trym home where she kept her antiquities, 1890

Here in a tin box are specimens of actual food offerings deposited 3,000 years ago in various tombs at Thebes – shrivelled dates, lentils, nuts and even a slice of bread. Rings, necklaces, bracelets, ear-rings, armlets, mirrors and toilet objects once the delight of dusky beauties long since embalmed and forgotten … And there are stranger things than these … here is a baby's foot (some mother cried over it once) in the Japanese cabinet in the ante-room. There are three mummied hands behind the dictionary in the library and there are two arms with hands complete – the one almost black, the other singularly fair, in a drawer in my dressing room, and grimmest of all, I have the heads of two ancient Egyptians in a wardrobe in my bedroom.

TAKING THE LAW IN ONE'S OWN HANDS.

Fair but Considerate Customer. "PRAY SIT DOWN. YOU LOOK SO TIRED. I'VE BEEN RIDING ALL THE AFTERNOON IN A CARRIAGE, AND DON'T REQUIRE A CHAIR."

A *Punch*-eye view of Victorian shopping.

8 – Going shopping

GOING SHOPPING AT THE BEGINNING OF QUEEN VICTORIA'S REIGN mostly meant shopping in the Bristol markets, or buying from street traders, at least as far as food was concerned. Shops were then concentrated in the centre of the city. By the end of the century, however, thanks to the building boom and public transport, shopping had been transformed: each suburb had an amazing array of small shops. High Street, Wine Street and Castle Street had become what we would call a shopping precinct.

The sheer diversity of goods produced as a result of the Industrial Revolution and mechanisation, and the trade with the colonies, meant that a Victorian Bristolian could buy literally everything under the sun, from a papier mâché piano to a solar topee, from French corsets to velocipedes. What we call retail therapy was invented by the Victorians, who also invented the department store, the chain store and mail order.

In 1837 Bristol, protectionism had ended, and 'foreigners' were no longer prevented from trading in any goods, anywhere in the city. There were almost daily food markets, for meat, poultry, fish, cheese, vegetables and flowers, the latter two grown locally in a city which still had vast stretches of market gardens from Barton Hill to Frenchay and Stapleton. The more specialised trades – the bakers, confectioners, drapers, tailors, jewellers – sold from shops. By 1901, Bristol still had markets, but much of the population had moved out to the surburbs, and all the major arteries of the city, the Hotwells Road, Whiteladies Road, Stapleton Road, Redcliffe Street, East Street, Bedminster, Gloucester Road, Wells Road, were lined with small shops, each serving a small local community.

By modern standards, Victorian Bristol was vastly over-shopped, with each shopping street boasting half a dozen each of butchers, grocers, greengrocers and bakers. Without refrigeration, food shopping had to be done daily and most people walked to the shops, so they needed them nearby. In poorer districts, second-hand shops, and shops which gave credit, were needed, and shops sold ready-cooked food for families without cooking facilities. In most areas itinerant merchants would cry their wares in the street, selling from a tray or barrow pies, muffins, cakes, sweets, ices and fruit.

For all but the posh, who shopped in Clifton Village, Queen's Road and Park Street, the Saturday treat was the visit to the Castle Street area, which from the 1870s was the Victorian equivalent of Broadmead, with late-night opening, closure to traffic, and a fashion parade and supper thrown in.

The department store arrived in the middle of the century. Thomas Jones, the Welsh draper, opened a shop in Wine Street in 1843, and sold whatever he could lay his hands on, from cheese and beer to silks and satins, brooms and baskets, and he was famous for his wild window displays. He kept buying new premises and in 1863 moved into 56–63 Wine Street, describing himself as a wholesale and retail silk mercers, drapers and haberdashers, agents for Tetley's pale ale and dealer in Cumberland hams.

By 1875, he advertised the store as selling general drapery goods, furniture, carpets, bedsteads and bedding 'and every requisite for house furnishing, doing all our business for ready Money, and buying direct from the Manufacturers enables us to offer most Fashionable goods at the Lowest possible Prices.' Jones listed 50 departments, which included mantles, mourning goods, furs, stays, boots, bonnets and hosiery.

Jones established the important business principle, soon to be copied by other astute traders, of fixed prices, cash only, and no credit. It was the Victorian habit to haggle over prices, and in middle-class areas, shoppers got credit as a matter of course.

His was the first department store, but eventually there were four more: Cordeux opened at Merchants Road and Regent Street, in Clifton, in the 1860s, Jolly opened his Bristol branch in 1858 at College Green, Baker Baker set up in Bridge Street in the 1880s and J. F. Taylor on College Green in the 1870s.

Shopping arcades were very successful in London, but not in Bristol. Architect Joseph King built two, one in Whiteladies Road (the remains of it can be seen above the Vittoria pub) and the perfectly preserved Clifton Arcade in Boyce's Avenue, now serving exactly the purpose for which it was built. Both ventures failed, because King failed to attract retailers to rent the units. The Clifton Arcade in 1880 became Knee's Pantechnicon, and was used for furniture storage, and it then remained closed to the public for over a century. The only successful shopping arcades were the architecturally rather splendid Upper and Lower Arcades in Broadmead, one of which survives to this day (the other was destroyed in the Blitz).

Chain stores were a later development: the Co-op set the trend for food chains when it opened in St Paul's in 1884; the movement was founded to supply the poor with cheap unadulterated food in an age when a lack of inspection made it possible to sell all kinds of lines bulked out and coloured by often dangerous additions, like alum in flour, and lead oxide in wine. Regulation did not come until 1879 with the Sale of Food and Drugs Act.

Others copied the Co-op: locally Shirley's and Budgett's grocery stores were in effect chains, for they had several branches, to compete with national chains like Sainsbury's and Liptons; another highly successful grocer was James Harding Mills, who in 1899 had six shops, which half a century later became the nucleus of the national chain of supermarkets, Gateway, now Somerfield.

But it was the small shops that dominated the shopping scene. In a typical street like Whiteladies Road, or East Street, Bedminster, apart from all the food shops, you would find several booksellers, ironmongers, shoe shops, drapers, haberdashers, sellers of oil and coal, wallpaper; you would also find the service trades – estate agents, dressmakers, milliners, photographers, watchmakers, builders, plumbers, hairdressers, painters and

Castle Street, the hub of Victorian shopping in Bristol.

CORDEUX'S FOR NOVELTIES!   BUSES ALWAYS RUNNING.

JOHN CORDEUX & SONS, LTD., CLIFTON.

Leave
Zetland
Road,

10.30,
11.30,
12.30,
2.30,
3.30,
4.30.

Leave
Blackboy
Hill,

10.30,
11.30,
12.30,
2.30,
3.30,
4.30.

Return at

11, 12, 1, 3,
4, 5.

Cordeux's: the fashionable department store in the heart of Clifton.

decorators, and each of these would be a family-owned business, usually with the owner living above the shop.

For the shopper, there was bewildering choice, and because there was so much competition, shops vied with each other to cut prices and stay open the latest. So the life of the shop assistant was hard: in some businesses it meant a seven-year apprenticeship and living in – at Cordeux's in Regent Street, Clifton, some staff lived above the shop departments. Some employers would pay their staff wages in kind, with goods from the shop, or with tickets for goods from neighbouring traders, instead of cash, until the Truck Acts of the 1870s stopped the practice.

The hours, until regulated by law in 1886, were pretty much what the shop-keeper dictated, and staff were expected to come in before opening time, and to stay after closing time, cleaning and tidying up. Even the reforms still meant long hours: in 1891, the working hours of women and children were limited to 74 a week, and in 1892 it became illegal for anyone under 18 to work more than those hours. Men normally worked 80 to 90 hours a week, and even by the time Queen Victoria died, early closing was not obligatory. The pay was poor, but working conditions were considered better than in domestic service or in the factories, and there was the possibility of promotion.

The way shops were used has changed too. While we take it for granted that only big stores and chains will deliver, in Victorian times everyone, down to the smallest green-grocer's, would deliver, because they would not get custom otherwise. In working-class areas, the housewives would carry what they bought, but no mistress of a middle-class household would walk the streets carrying bags of fish or groceries. The system was

Chemist's
shop, High
Street by
Archibald
Ponton and
William Venn
Gough.
[*The Builder*,
October,
1869]

Apple seller at corner of Peter Street and Church Lane.

HATS AND BONNETS OF 1888.
MID-WINTER.

DRESS: IN SEASON AND IN REASON.
BY A LADY DRESSMAKER.

What the fashionable Victorian lady was wearing in 1888. [*The Girl's Own Paper*]

that the mistress went shopping and picked what she wanted, and left an order. This was either delivered, or she sent a servant to fetch it. The cook would either pay for the food delivered, or the shop would send an account once a month.

What the mistress of the house would spend a lot of time shopping for was clothes. Fashions of the time were elaborate and demanding – society expected women to have morning gowns, tea gowns, visiting outfits and evening outfits, all worn in the course of one day. While the poor relied on second-hand clothes bought from dress agencies, like Madam Virtue's, or second-hand shops and pawn shops, the middle classes had their clothes made for them – ready-to-wear was considered very downmarket, even for men, though the invention of the three-piece suit is credited to a Bristol tailoring firm, Coles and Pottow. Ready-made clothing, like that made by the Bristol firm of Wathen Gardiner, was for export, or for the working classes.

If the family did not employ a dressmaker, and there were over 300 to choose from in Bristol – it being a genteel occupation for respectable women – they could go to a shop such as The Alexandra (now Alexandra Workwear) or Cordeux and study patterns, and choose fabrics, and the shop's seamstresses would make it up, often in an amazingly short time. Only items such as shawls, hats, gloves and some shoes, and children's and baby-wear were bought ready-made; school uniforms would be bought from a firm like Steer and Geary in Clifton or Marsh's of Whiteladies Road. Choosing underwear was another elaborate ritual: it was available ready-made but the most fashionable women either sewed their own or had it made for them.

Caring for clothes was another big operation. While maids would brush and sponge and press outerwear every day, and hand-wash underwear and baby linen, the elaborate dresses, made in non-washable, shrinkable fabrics whose dyes were not fast, had to go to the dry-cleaners. This entailed having the garments unpicked and taken to pieces, cleaned in spirit (usually turps) and then re-assembled. Firms such as Brooks or Willways would do this, and also 'turn' garments by re-making them inside out. They were also dyers, and with the high mortality rate, spent much of their time dying clothes black, for the long obligatory mourning period. Richer folk could go to a mourning warehouse and buy outfits for the entire family, including children and servants.

And then this was the age of the corset. Since fashion demanded an hour-glass shape, Bristol had several famous corsetry manufacturers, such as Bayer, Chappell Allen and Langridge as well as a great many corsetry retailers. The array of styles was enormous, with corsets for daytime, evening, cycling, or tennis, and French styles were particularly sought after. Even young girls were put into corsets or 'improvers' which were designed to correct posture and prevent stooping – Charles Cross of Hallatrow produced one in 1871.

The other big Bristol fashion industry was of course footwear. While the bulk of the trade was in boots and men's shoes, high-fashion shoes were produced by firms like Denham Bros, or Brightmans, who hand-made elegant walking boots with rows of buttons and suede trim and glittery diamanté buckles. Plainer items, mostly made-to-measure, could be bought from the staggering number of shoemakers and retailers in the city. In 1899, some 500 were listed in the street directory – some of them with names not long vanished: Lennards, Goodenough, and Massingham.

Victorian businesses which are still trading in Bristol today include Earl and Chilcott, the jewellers, Veal's fishing tackle, Alexandra, Jones department store (taken over by Debenhams), W.H. Smith, Pickfords, Buxton the chemist, Bromheads the photographer, Brooks the dry cleaners (now Johnsons), Singer sewing machines, the Co-op, Garaway the nursery, and Dunscombe the optician.

Sports became popular in the second half of the century and sports outfitters and equipment suppliers did good business, for an outfit was needed for every sport, and especially for women, who had to dress suitably for tennis, croquet, archery, cricket, cycling and golf. Shops opened to cater for all the new Victorian hobbies, music, gardening, collecting, photography, needlework, or art. If there was a demand, a shop arrived to meet it. Modern shopaholics would have adored shopping in Victorian Bristol.

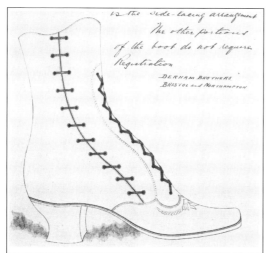

Lady's lace-up ankle boot from Derham Bros of Bristol, 1891.

Snapshots of shopping

The vegetable stalls are mostly kept by Kingswood women – children of that rude race which Wesley with his meek yet indomitable spirit, strove to evangelise. There they stand, handling Brobdignagian cabbages and watering drooping radishes in the self-same old-fashioned dress in which their great-grandmothers attired themselves; the hat they wear is of black felt, the wide leaves of which are bent down to cover the ears, and the shallow rounded crown is encircled with puffing of black ribbon; under the head-covering peeps the plaited white cap, and the hair is dressed in an infinite number of small thin loops which form a fringe as it were across the forehead.
From The Land We Live In, c.1840

A fashionable wedding at Christ Church Clifton, 1859

The bride wore a dress of rich white taffeta glace, with double skirt ornamented with tulle illusion and ruches of taffeta, high bodice, the sleeves very wide and open, trimmed with ruches of taffeta and edged with quilted ribbon, with full illusion sleeves under. An elegant blonde veil entirely covered the whole dress.

A Noble Connection

Patronised by the Duke of Beaufort, J. Brooks, Dyer, tends his grateful acknowledgments to the Nobility, Clergy and Gentry for the liberal support with which they have honoured him and begs to inform them that he has removed to Nelson Place (opposite his former establishment) where he hopes for continuance of their patronage.
Advertisement, 1865 (Nelson Place was in Princess Victoria Street)

How To Shop

It is not enough to have plenty of money; one must try to become a really clever buyer. A 'clever' buyer is not one who beats down the price of every article until she is well known, and prices are put up to come down to their smallest value only. She must know the real value of every article at each season of the year, and either give that exact value or know how to go without gracefully, or to make up by purchasing an equivalent at less cost.

A neatly bound Account Book of oblong shape, an ivory slate and pencil and a card and pencil in the purse is the whole stock-in-trade of an account-keeper. The account book is kept in the mistress's Davenport, the slate hangs up in the kitchen and the card and purse are naturally in the pocket. Every time any money is spent enter the item at once on the card, which is kept in place in the purse by an elastic passed over it. Every Saturday remove the card and insert a fresh one, copying the list on the card into the account book.

Every Saturday morning receive the Household Books from the cook, who hands the slate, on which she had marked the sums paid at the kitchen door for sundries and parcels not put down in the weekly books; this statement includes all extras. To this add the housekeeping expenses: butcher, baker, milkman, grocer, greengrocer, washing etc., and add this up.

Mrs Beeton's Everyday Cookery and Housekeeping Book, 1865

Food for One Person Weekly

Tea, two ounces, coffee, a quarter of a pound (if for breakfast only), cocoa paste, a quarter of a pound, for breakfast, sugar, half a pound, cheese, half a pound, butter, half a pound, milk, one quart, bread, eight pounds for a woman, sixteen pounds for a man or a boy, meat, six pounds, beer, one gallon for a woman, seven quarts for a man, potatoes, three and a half pounds. A large supply of vegetables, fish or puddings will reduce the scale of meat.

The mistress of a family should ascertain the price of every article of food in her neighbourhood, as prices differ with localities, and that which might be economical food in one place is frequently the reverse in another. In order to learn the prices, she must not disdain to market for herself, if she is her own housekeeper. She will thus be able by personal observation to learn which are the best shops for different articles and what are the fair rates of payment for them.

Warne's Everyday Cookery, 1875

Trapnell's furnishing showroom, 1875

The showrooms (in College Green) connected with the establishment are the largest in the West of England and contain suites of Apartments together with an extensive collection of Modern and Medieval furniture, carpets and upholstery goods.

To the furnishing of residences for the Clergy and for Professional Gentlemen a special department is devoted and lists prepared at totals varying from £60 for the house complete, to £700.

The same firm were the Designers and Manufacturers of the costly casket of ebony and boxwood, which contained the jewels presented by the citizens of Bristol, to HRH the Princess of Wales on the occasion of her marriage.

Opening advertisement for King's Arcade, Boyces Avenue, Clifton, April 10, 1879

Bristol and Clifton Bazaar and Winter Gardens now open. Situated near the Clifton Suspension Bridge with entrances in King's Road and Boyce's Avenue, Victoria Square.

The building, which is designed and erected by Mr Joseph William King of this city, at a cost of over £10,500 is very convenient and elegant in appearance, well lighted, ventilated and heated with hot water and it is very commodious, having over 20,000 feet of floor space and the glass roof and other parts of the building are very artistically arranged with Virgin Cork, Ferns, creeping Plants and Moss, to which will shortly be added Tropical and other Plants and Shrubs, Fountains in play, Choice Fish, English and Foreign Birds etc., which will present a very cheerful and agreeable appearance.

It has a GRAND RESTAURANT where refreshments may always be had at a low tariff. There are also Private Retiring Rooms and lavatories.

A choice assortment of Flowers in Pots, or cut for Bouquets etc., always on sale. Spaces may be had for the Exhibition of Mechanical and other modes.

SHOPS to be LET, with immediate possession, for Fancy Businesses. For particulars apply at the Premises.

A Celebrated BAND is engaged to Play Every SATURDAY from three o'clock until nine pm.

Save our trees

Sir, I must protest at the wanton destruction of trees in the enclosure adjoining Boyce's Avenue. It was previously one of the most charming parts of Clifton before the ruthless felling. And what for? To build shops. We do not need more shops.

Letter to Clifton Chronicle, 1878

Lesser Columbus on corsets, 1893

Now in dealing with the use of the corset, one must disassociate it from its abuse under the name of tight lacing. It is particularly reserved to our own time to demonstrate that the two things are not synonymous. Distortion is not beautiful, but the fine figure girl of the present time is. The perfect corset is a much to be commended thing. It supports the figure, gives it artistic curves and keeps out the cold.

Expensive Clifton

I see that a first class butcher in St Michael's Hill is selling best joints of beef at 9d a pound. Can you tell me how it is that in Clifton butchers still keep the prices as high as 10 $^1/_2$d for the same joints?

Clifton Chronicle, 1880

Best-selling titles, 1880

Ventriloquism made Easy; The Etiquette Companion; Courtship and Matrimony; Pedestrianism; Elementary Gymnastics; Modern Outdoor Amusements; Fun and Flirtation Forfeits; Flora Symbolica, or the Language of Flowers; The Happy Home Songster; 62 Stories of Brave Deeds.

Cordeux advertisement, 1880

John Cordeux and Sons' business which was commenced scarce 20 years ago with only about seven yards of counter in a very small shop has grown day by day in Public Favour until now Ladies can ask for almost anything with the certainty of having the want supplied.

Description of John Cordeux's department stores, 1890s

A lordly treasure house; a tour of inspection through the numerous departments is like a visit to one of the most gorgeous bazaars of the Orient. Agencies in every part of the globe contribute to the lavish display.

SION BOARDING HOUSE,
WITH LODGING HOUSES adjoining, FACING THE DOWNS,
CLIFTON,
HAS BEEN ESTABLISHED EIGHTY YEARS.

Conducted by Mrs. Minifie.

HOT & COLD BATHS, GOOD STABLING, &c.

C. MINIFIE,
SHIRT TAILOR, HOSIER, & GLOVER,
36, COLLEGE GREEN, BRISTOL.

LADIES', GENTLEMEN'S, AND CHILDREN'S HOSIERY,
GLOVES, CRAVATS, UNDER-CLOTHING, &c.
DRESSING GOWNS,
SHIRTS, COLLARS, STOCKS, AND BRACES,
UMBRELLAS, WATER-PROOF COATS,
CAPES, FISHING STOCKINGS, &c.

Directions to Measure for Minifie's Registered Coat-Sleeve Shirt sent,
and all Parcels Carriage free.

SHOW ROOMS
For Ladies and Children, for every description of Linen, Long Cloth,
and warm Under-Clothing, Dressing Gowns, Morning Wrappers,
Riding Collars, &c. &c.

Wedding Orders and India Outfits. Baby Linen.

HENRY B. WILLETT,
ENGRAVER AND PRINTER,
1, ST. STEPHEN'S AVENUE,
CLARE STREET, BRISTOL.

Brass and Zinc Door, Office, Window, and Warehouse Plates made and
engraved in the first style.
MONUMENTAL AND CHURCH BRASSES ENGRAVED AND ILLUMINATED.
•.• Engraving and Printing of every description.
32

DIAL HOUSE,
18, BROADMEAD, BRISTOL.

THOMAS BALE,
WORKING WATCH & CLOCK MAKER
OPTICIAN,
JEWELLER, GOLD AND SILVERSMITH,
HAS ON SALE A CHOICE ASSORTMENT OF
Silver and Silver-Plated Breakfast and Tea Services, Waiters, Cake
Baskets, Toast Racks, Candlesticks, &c.
English and Foreign Weight and Spring Clocks, Dials, &c.
Gold and Silver Watches, with the latest improvements.
Gold and Silver Guards, Pencil Cases, Snuff and Scent Boxes.
Barometers, Telescopes, and Mathematical Instruments.
ELECTRO-PLATE FORKS, SPOONS, &c.
Watches, Clocks, Jewellery, Plate and Plated Articles
neatly repaired, at moderate charges.
T. B. has one of the largest Stocks of Spectacles and Eye Glasses in
the City, to suit every defect of sight.
Spectacle Glasses of every sight and color, fitted into frames.

SMITH AND CO.
CARPET AND FURNISHING
WAREHOUSEMEN,
No. 13, ST. AUGUSTINE'S PARADE,
Opposite the Drawbridge,
BRISTOL.

A SPLENDID ASSORTMENT OF PAPER HANGINGS.

CLIFTON TURTLE DEPÔT,
Patronized by the Duke of Beaufort.

WARREN,
Cook and Confectioner, Fruiterer, &c.
5, REGENT PLACE, CLIFTON.

DINNERS, BREAKFASTS, BALLS, ROUTS, ETC. SUPPLIED.
33

A meeting of ladies to promote the Early Closing Movement

The undersigned, in view of the great physical and moral evils resulting to so many young men and women in this city from the practice of shops being kept open till late hours, feeling that if there were no late customers the shops would not be kept open, would earnestly recommend their fellow-citizens to abstain from the practice of shopping after 4 o'clock on Saturdays, and after 7 o'clock on other days of the week.

Working girls

The shop girls' hours of labour are excessive – from 8am to 8pm on five days of the week, and 8 to 12 on Saturdays; with no time for mental or moral improvement or for social intercourse and necessary outdoor exercise, what inducement do they have to be good and how can they be healthy in mind and body?

Letter to Clifton Chronicle, 1887

Elegant Clifton

Without Clifton Bristol would take a lower rank in the social scale. From Clifton the busy city daily receives an influx of residents and visitors who bring with them evidence of the brightness and freshness of a purer atmosphere and associations which bespeak the refinement and elegance to be found only in a fashionable neighbourhood. The business houses of Clifton are of necessity very high class.

Where to buy in Bristol or Clifton, An Illustrated Trades Review, 1890

Grocery wars, 1896–97

Every possible opportunity was taken by those jealous of the progress of the Co-operative stores to discredit its operations. The neighbourhoods of Totterdown and Bedminster were flooded with anti-Co-operative literature; enterprising grocers posed before the community as universal benefactors; comparisons were drawn between the goods they sold and presumably similar goods sold by the Society, of course much in favour of their own.

Industrial Co-operation in Bristol

A Dishonest Employee

For some time the affairs of the Newfoundland Road branch of the Co-operative Society had been more or less unsatisfactory. The quarter ending December 1889 has shown a loss which no-one had been able to explain satisfactorily. Six months later it was discovered that the Manager there had been embezzling the Society's money. Attempting to cover his defalcations, he filled tea chests with bricks and mortar, taking them into stock as so many chests of tea. He was prosecuted and at the hearing it transpired that he had been gambling and associating himself with loose characters. It was estimated that through him the Society lost upwards of £50.

Industrial Co-operation in Bristol

Victorian brand names still around in 2005

Fry's Cocoa, Beecham's Pills, Dr Collis Brown's chlorodine mixture, Parrish's Food, Wills cigars, Harvey's Bristol Cream, Bovril, Pears soap, Syrup of Figs, and Hovis.

Victorian inventions advertised in Bristol newspapers included

Electric towels and hairbrushes, Claxton's Ear Cap for Prominent Ears, Dr. Gordon's Elegant Pills for fatness, the Invigorator Belt; Death in the boot for lack of O'Brien's Patent Galoshes, Aid for Ringworm, a Mother's Dread, the Harness Eye Battery, Train your moustache the way it should go with Carter's Thixaline. Wear Armstrong's Jubilee braces!

A fashion note

The lady cyclist has evidently found room for an additional ornament in her toilet, owing to the abbreviated nature of the costume most serviceable for cycling. Her skirts are just short enough to display a massive gold cable chain just above her right ankle!

Letter to Clifton Chronicle, 1895

Victorian mourning costumes, as advertised in *Sylvia's Home Journal*, 1879.

9 – In sickness and in health

IF YOU LIVED IN BRISTOL IN 1837, unless you were rich your chances of living to a ripe old age, or of your children living beyond the age of five, were poor. Bristol was one of the most unhealthy cities in the country, and as late as 1850, nearly half the children born died before they reached their fifth year, and the mortality rate was 28 per 1,000. A child's burial was cheap – one of the many undertakers could arrange one for as little as £3.50, plus £1 for the plot and £7 for a monument.

The city was hit by epidemic after epidemic – of cholera, typhoid, scarlet fever, diphtheria and smallpox, and the biggest killer of all was tuberculosis. Where you lived dictated survival: when typhus swept through the city in 1864, there were cases in nearly every house in St Jude's; in all 1,500 caught it, and 150 died. With little understanding of how diseases were spread, or of disinfection and anti-sepsis methods, and few efficient drugs, medicine could do little. In any case, treatment was available only to those who could pay for it.

(Sexually transmitted diseases were rife, too, thanks to the flourishing underworld of prostitution, carried on mainly in St Philips. The only treatments, usually using mercury, were primitive and painful, and not very effective, so that innocent brides of all classes were infected by their husbands, who had resorted to quack remedies for a cure.)

The reason why Bristol was such an unhealthy city could be smelled everywhere; the water supply was polluted, the River Frome through the city was the receptacle for sewage, the streets were full of rotting rubbish, and the poor lived in slums without any sanitation. Even the wealthy living in grand houses in Clifton had to deal with the stink of cess-pits and raw sewage running through the streets. If householders wanted clean safe water from a spring, they had to buy it at a penny for two small buckets.

What changed Bristol from being one of the least healthy big cities to one of the most healthy by the end of the century, was an ambitious programme to provide clean water, and to build a new sewage system, and a new understanding of how disease was spread and how to prevent it. From 1851, when the programme started, 150 miles of new sewers were to be built by the 1880s, and the mortality rate declined steadily.

The catalyst for all this reform was the Public Health Report of 1845, by Sir Henry de la Beche and Dr Lyon Playfair. Of their visit to inspect Bristol, they wrote: 'In Clifton, although chiefly composed of handsome houses inhabited by persons of Affluent and easy circumstances, the want of proper sewage is deplorable. Ranges of handsome houses, otherwise well-appointed, have nothing but a system of cesspools – often the holes from which the stones for building the house have been taken.'

The shared awfulness – and disease – of a Victorian slum.

Dr William Budd, the great
pioneer of preventative medicine.

They reported that the few sewers which ran along Royal York Crescent, Sion Hill and Princes Buildings ended by going over the edge of the Avon gorge, where the contents dropped into the river. If wealthy Clifton was this badly served, the state of the centre of Bristol must have been unimaginable.

The hero in Bristol's Victorian public health improvement was Dr William Budd, who had ideas about preventative medicine well before the rest of his profession, and made the connection between living conditions, sanitary arrangements and ill health. Budd had done his own inspections in 1845.

He visited a family – father, mother and six children – living in a basement in a court in Lewin's Mead:

'How long have you lived here?'

'Nearly two years.'

'Have you enjoyed good health since then?'

'No, all our troubles have come upon us here. I used to be strong and lusty, able for work; but now am weak and sickly. I have had many children and never suffered from my confinements until I came to this place, but since then I have had two dead-born children. But what distresses so much is that my children who were healthy before, are becoming very puny, and my husband is not able for the work he used to do. God has dealt hardly with us for two years.'

'Is the smell from the privy always as bad as it is now?'

'Generally much worse. Mr. – the missionary when he comes to visit us, often has to put his head out of the window, he gets so faint, I think sometimes that we are all worse when the smell gets worse.'

In his evidence to the Health of Towns Commission Budd told the inspectors that houses along the Frome had privies discharging directly into the water. 'These privies hang over a bank of mud which is only swept at spring tide or when the Frome is swollen with freshets [floodwater]. The state of things in the interval is too loathsome and disgusting to describe.'

Budd, who became in everything but name the city's first medical officer of health, had himself suffered typhoid and as he toured the slums of St Philips and Redcliffe he observed the closeness of the water supply to the privies, and made the connection that the disease was carried through the contamination of the water supply, though his theory was ridiculed by the medical establishment. But he was proved right in 1866, when another cholera epidemic arrived; he ordered disinfection of streets, courts, yards, privies, drains and sewers with sulphate of iron, and the cleaning of all pump handles, and it worked. Only 29 died and half of those lived outside the city. In the 1849 epidemic, nearly 450 had died.

Budd knew that the ultimate key to public health improvement was the provision of a clean water supply, which arrived when Bristol Waterworks was set up in 1846. Before then, the water supply was dirty and inadequate. An 1840 report on the city said:

> Viewed as a sanitary question, there are few if any large towns in England in which the supply of water is so inadequate as in Bristol. The labour and consequent expense attached to the system of obtaining a supply of water from the draw-wells or pumps engenders filthy habits and directly acting upon the health and indirectly, the morals of the people. The labour of fetching water leads to a very sparing use of it.

By 1866, nearly every house in the city had a supply of Bristol Waterworks Company water, though as late as the 1870s builders were still digging wells in the new suburbs such as Redland. Moreover, householders had to be able to afford the water charges; with a house rent of £5 a year, the charge was 1s. 3d. a quarter, for a £10 annual rent, the charge was 10s. Naturally slum landlords were reluctant to pay up.

Impure water was not the only source of infection; outbreaks were often traced to dairies and slaughterhouses. The poor bought second-hand clothing which carried fleas, lice and germs, and the sanitary improvements that brought better health to the middle classes did not extend to the poor, who lived in slums with one privy to 16 houses. In 1851 a Sanitary Committee was set up and one of its tasks was to force slum landlords to put in new privies. In 1857 a Mr Frederick Bull of Bedminster was ordered to remove an offensive privy and put two new ones in its place, with pipes connecting them to the new sewer pipe. Proper street cleaning and the regular collection of refuse, which came

Leonard Lane, skirting the old city wall between Small Street and Corn Street.

in the 1860s, was another weapon in the fight.

Then there was the stinking Frome to deal with – a source of infection for the people who lived alongside it, as a St Philip's resident pointed out to the Corporation in a letter to the *Bristol Times* in 1854. 'There's cholera a-coming and the stink under my windows is worse than ever. I lives in front of the Frome and I say the stink is a shame … I should

The Frome before it was covered over.

main like his Worships the Mayor to come and smell it of a Sunday, if it didn't do he good, perhaps 'twould the city.'

Refuse collection was another step towards improving public health. By 1872 'scavenging' was being carried out by private contractors appointed by the Sanitary Authority; they cleansed and swept the principal thoroughfares daily, and other streets two or three times a week; the scavengers also removed ashes from iron boxes in the street, though it was reported that these had become 'stinking and offensive' because householders added cabbage, fish and garbage as well.

Keeping the body clean was another problem. For the poor, there was no means of bathing, and when the first public bath-house opened on Rope Walk in Hotwells, in 1850, 7,352 people used the facilities in the first four weeks. Slipper baths opened at Broad Weir the same year were equally well used.

Eventually all these measures worked, and the mortality rate dropped steadily, from 226 per 1,000 in 1876 to 179 per 1,000 in 1883, and the figure kept falling throughout the century.

But an abiding problem was the ability to pay for treatment if you became ill. And even if you could pay, the repertoire of drugs to fight what were generally called 'fevers' was very limited. The poorer you were, the more likely you were to die, noted Dr William Kay, physician to the Clifton Dispensary. 'The mortality of tradespeople is more than treble the mortality among the higher classes.'

Quack treatments, heavily advertised in the local press, were designed to avoid a costly visit to the doctor. You could buy Dover's Powders, Daffy's Elixir, Black Drops,

Batley's Sedative, made from wormwood and herbs infused in beer, Parr's Life Pills, Norris's Drops for colds and fevers, made from emetic tartar and spirits of wine with vegetable dye.

Claims were made that these medicines cured everything but in fact they cured nothing and most contained sedatives to suppress symptoms. Laudanum was a universal remedy. In the latter half of the century there was also a mania for health gadgets, exercisers, posture correctors, electrical treatments and electro-magnetic underwear.

The city's medical institutions had to cope when these treatments failed. The Bristol Infirmary had been set up in 1737 and became the Royal Infirmary in 1850; Bristol Medical School was opened in 1833, the General Hospital in 1854, and the Children's Hospital in 1866. There had been private lunatic asylums since the eighteenth century, notably Dr Fox's at Brislington, but the first city-run asylum for the mentally ill opened at Fishponds in 1851.

There were also the voluntary institutions, set up to help the poor; the oldest, dating from 1812, was the Clifton Dispensary in Dowry Square; Redland got one in 1860, and from 1874 there was the Read Dispensary, set up specifically for women and children. A Vaccine Institution which treated poor children for sixpence opened in 1838, and an Eye Dispensary dated from 1812. The destitute poor were cared for on the rates, at St Peter's Hospital. The Blind Asylum had been opened in 1834 and the Deaf and Dumb Asylum in 1841.

Some voluntary institutions charged small sums, to cover costs, with a rebate if the patient came back for a check-up, while others were supported by subscribers, who each had tickets to give to deserving cases – which meant that the sick had to make the rounds to get a sick note entitling them to free treatment.

In a mid-Victorian Bristol hospital, conditions were not conducive to survival. The surgeon wore a top hat to see patients and kept his ordinary coat on for minor operations; when undertaking a major operation he exchanged this for an old black cloth coat kept for the purpose. A row of these dirty garments might be seen hanging up in the consulting room, ready for use. The food was meant to be nourishing: a pint of milk, and soup made from the dinner remains of the previous day …

Bristol lays claim to the first British woman doctor, Elizabeth Blackwell, who lived in the city as a child but qualified and worked in the United States. A more local female medical heroine was Eliza Walker Dunbar who qualified at the University of Zurich in 1872 and the following year won a post as Resident Medical Officer at the Hospital For Women and Children on St Michael's Hill. She was very much the token woman doctor and soon ruffled male feathers and was forced out, thereby attracting national publicity.

For as *The Lancet* said, 'Women are neither physically or morally qualified for many of the onerous, important and confidential duties of the general practitioner; nor capable of the prolonged exertions or severe exposures to all kinds of weather which a profession-al life entail.' Eliza devoted herself to the provision of services for women and children, staffed by women, and became the first Medical Attendant of the Read Dispensary.

Another need was filled by Ada Vachell, who, seeing the lack of provision for crip-pled and disabled children, started the Guild of The Handicapped to provide them with therapy, education and recreation.

By the time the Queen died, medicine in Bristol was far better organised, standards of care were much higher, and the range of medicines and surgical techniques available far more sophisticated. There was a nationwide move towards more free treatment in hos-pitals, but the fact remained that for more than another 40 years, when the National Health Service was created, only the well-off could afford to be ill in Bristol.

The high mortality rates in the Victorian period are echoed by the numbers of under-takers in the city. There were 67 in 1851, when ill health was at its peak. Since death was common, rituals had to be devised to deal with the grief; one was the elaborate funeral with black plumes hired from the feather funeral men, and strings of mutes in top hats, with black crepe bands round them, and an expensive coffin – and the other was extended and ostentatious mourning.

Bristol drapers made a living out of mourning and in the 1860s there were three mourning warehouses in the city, so that an entire household, if you could afford it, could be fitted out in the latest fashion. Those who could not afford new mourning clothes went to a dyer like Brooks, to have their entire wardrobe dyed black. Death was big business.

There was also mourning stationery to be bought, and black gloves and black-edged handkerchiefs, mourning jewellery made from jet, or the hair of the deceased. (A Bristol firm displayed its hair jewellery at the Great Exhibition of 1851) Queen Victoria's own protracted mourning for Prince Albert set the duration of grief, and there were set times of mourning, according to the closeness of the dead person.

The rule was two years for a husband, and then lavender or purple could be worn by the widow; children wore black for six months (they even had black ribbons in their under-wear) and then white. Parents were mourned for a year and even quite distant relations by marriage were supposed to be mourned for six weeks. It went without saying that during that time there would be no dinner parties, or dances or entertainments. In fact mourning and funerals became so excessive and expensive that in the early 1880s a Mourning Reform Association was formed – hence the Bristol undertakers who adver-tised 'reform funerals'.

The size of Bristol's Victorian cemeteries and the elaborate monuments they contained are witness to both the high death rate and the way people dealt with bereavement. The city parishes' graveyards were full by the time of Bristol's population boom, and they were forced by law to close in 1854. It was clear that either private companies, or the city itself, would have to create large cemeteries to cope. Cremation did not become legal until after Queen Victoria died, and without embalming, bodies had to be buried within two days, so undertakers often worked flat out.

Arno's Vale cemetery was laid out in 1836, and extended three times to hold the 100,000 burial plots needed by the end of the nineteenth century. It was the place where the great and the good most wished to have their monument. Greenbank cemetery, where at the end of the Queen's reign a 'first class grave, with exclusive right of further burials for a period of 75 years' cost £6, was consecrated in 1871. Cremation, legalised in 1902, brought an end to the over-crowded Victorian cemeteries, which have now become something to cherish, as shown by the current restoration of Arno's Vale: a perfect illustration of Bristol's way of death in Victoria's reign. (See *Arno's Vale Cemetery* by Lesley Turney, to be published by Redcliffe Press in 2006)

Snapshots of Health

Medical Assistance at 18, College Street, 1842

To those who are suffering from venereal or syphilitic diseases and of all diseases arising from solitary habits or excess. A practical treatise on the above distressing complaints with observations on the baneful effects of gonorrhoea, gleets and strictures, seminal weakness, impotency etc., with the most approved and safe mode of treatment and cure without confinement or interruption from business, is given with each box of the French Marone pills, price 2s. 9d, 4s. 6d., and 11s. each.

These pills are mild and effectual in their operation, without mercury or mineral and require no restraint of diet, loss of time or hindrance from business, possessing the power of eradicating every symptom of the disease in its worst stage without the least exposure to the patient; they are particularly recommended to be taken before by persons entering into the matrimonial state, lest the indiscretions of a parent are the source of vexation to him for the remainder of his existence.

There are many disorders of the generative system that are consequent upon the too free and indiscriminate indulgence of the passions exhibiting in some debility from excess, in others the relaxing effects of tropical climate and in many, indeed in too many, the various maladies which afflict the student, the misanthrope, the gay, the dissipated and the libertine. To all such then Dr Henry addresses himself offering hope, energy, muscular strength and felicity.

Advertisement in the Bristol Times, October 1842

Women's problems

Women who have been deceived by the misleading advertisements, testimonials and

Mayor's Paddock baths and wash-houses, Bedminster at the turn of the century, and, *below*, the washhouse superintendent with staff.

other worthless representations of Madames, Nurses, companies, doctors' widows etc. should send a stamped addressed envelope for my little book which tells you why these people fail to cure you. It explains in a scientific way HOW REGULARITY MAY BE RESTORED in a few hours without any discomfort.

Fits and nervous Complaints? Miss Pike's Powders

This invaluable medicine, for the care of EPILEPTIC, HYSTERIC and every other descriptions of FITS has for many years been gratuitously and successfully administered of the above lady; but in consequence of the increasing demand, and the earnest solicitation of friends, it is now offered to the public for sale. It had also proved highly serviceable on NERVOUS AFFECTATIONS OF THE HEAD, inducing mental weakness and (in some cases) bordering on insanity; and in the alleviation and cure of the various species of Nervous Complaints. No confinement or restraint, more than that of being very temperate, is necessary during its use, as it is perfectly harmless and a child might take it. 2s. 9d.

From Miss Pike, 15, Park Place, Clifton. Bristol Times, 1842

Report on conditions in the Out-Patients department at Bristol Royal Infirmary, 1848

On Monday and Thursday mornings at 11am there were four Physicians and five Surgeons. The atmosphere of the room in which the patients waited was described as tainted and poisonous; a policeman was employed to keep order and when a fresh batch was wanted, the door of the common room was opened by one or two attendants and the crowd of maimed and diseased wretches shouldered and fought their way into the place where they were seeing the Physicians and Surgeons who had to arrange and sort them as they came in. Men and women were admitted into the room where they were examined and attended to together and the great indelicacy of this arrangement was obvious.

Death in hospital, 1849

A poor soul who was shortly to die and knew it begged that when her time came she might hold the hand of the Ward Sister. The patient was conscious to the last; the Sister sat quietly and cheerfully by her side and held her hand. What she said to her I do not know, but the child (she was only 18) said that she was quite happy with the support of her friend and passed away declaring that she did not mind a bit. This surely better than frightening patients by handing out religious tracts.

A great nuisance

I take the liberty of addressing you on the subject of a great nuisance to which the whole of this city and especially my own parish has been subjected now for several years. I allude to a river called the Frome, which flows through the heart of the city and into which the sewage from several thousand houses discharges itself. This so called river is during summer months nearly stagnant and, as during a considerable portion of the course through the city it is uncovered, the stench that arises from it is positively intolerable.

Whenever cholera has appeared in Bristol, its virulence has been most evident along the course of this pestilential stream. Last year I drew up a memorial and obtained the signatures of 600 respectable householders to it and presented it to the town council who own a great portion of the river, as an earnest appeal to remedy the fatal nuisance complained of.

Some remedial plans were proposed yet no further notice has been taken. My parishioners are particularly affected by it for not only does the open river run behind their houses, obliging them to keep their windows closed during the summer, but it runs in front of their church so that the congregation have often during the summer months been detained in large numbers in the church in consequence of the offensive stench from the river … The evil has now risen to a fearful pitch and no remedy has been applied. The river should evidently be treated as a sewer and covered over where it traverses the city.

Letter to the Bristol Local Board of Health from the Vicar of St Matthias Church, the Rev A.C. Rowley, 1855

Death by consumption, 1859

[Eliza Anne Harris, a spoiled young Clifton girl, became a Christian after surviving cholera in 1854 and dropped the social round for good works, until she became ill again.] I am so thin that the bones are coming through my skin on the right side and I cannot lie on it, I cannot be on the left side because then I feel so sharp a pain through lying that it is like a sword pricking me. If I lie on my back I cannot breathe and I get so weary of sitting up.

William Budd on TB

The idea that phthsis is a self-propagated disease, and that all the leading phenomena of its distribution may be explained by supposing that it is disseminated through society by a specific germ contained in the tuberculous matter cast off by the persons already suffering from the disease, first came to my mind unbidden as it were, while I was walking on the Observatory Hill in Clifton in the second week of August, 1856.

Take medicine and die, apply Magnetic Currents and Live

Thousands of helpless invalids of all classes of society have now blazoned before them all the horrors of an inclement winter. Mr W. Wilson has found a method of attaching to clothing voltaic piles attached to magnets; he contends that these by absorbing the natural exudation of the skin give out a constant galvanic current and so keep up a continual supply of magnetism.

We supply corsets, vests, chest protectors, throat protectors, spine bands, friction gloves, pads, wristlets, knee caps, leg appliances, anklets, soles, and the Wilsonia Armour, a garment fashioned out of India rubber cloth; upon these are fastened copper and zinc eyelets, powerfully magnetised; attached to these are plates of copper and zinc through which is passed a piece of chemically prepared calico. The internal work is covered with another piece of waterproof cloth and fastened together by a solution of India rubber, over which is laid a piece of flannel. A testimonial: 'I have been suffering from rheumatic gout and consequently sleepless nights for about 15 years but now, thanks to the Belt I am recovered.'

The Wilsonia Depot, at the Royal Bazaar Winter Gardens, Clifton in 1879

An advance on the privy

Improved Earth Closets and Inodorous Commodes, 35s. unpainted, 55s. varnished, and superior in hygiene and efficiency to the water closet. The evils arising from the contamination of our rivers are so great that, sooner or later, some such remedy must be applied.

Bristol Implement Company of St Thomas Street advertisement, 1871

Report on Arno's Vale Cemetery, 1875

In this lovely leafy nook, our loved ones rest, as it is the great cemetery of the citizens; the variety and costliness of the monuments are something to be marvelled at, some of them being exquisite in taste and exceedingly appropriate. 'Here let me lie in a quiet spot, with the green turf o'er my head, far from the city's hum, the wordling's heavy tread; Where the free winds blow and the branches wave, and the songbirds sweetly sing, 'til every mourner exclaims "O death where is thy sting".'

Bristol and its Environs, 1875

Life during pregnancy

When a woman is about to become a mother, she ought to remember that another life of health or delicacy is dependent on the care she can take of herself; that all she does will inevitably affect her child, and that physically as well as mentally. We know it is utterly impossible for the wife of a labouring man to give up work, nor is it necessary. The back is made for its burthen and it would be just as injurious for the labourer's wife to give up her daily work as for the lady to take to sweeping her own carpets or cooking the dinner.

Advice to wives from Cassell's Household Guide, 1877

From a Sonnet on the Children's Hospital, by Canon H.D. Rawnsley, 1877

I passed from halls of gaiety to one
Where children languished, tiny girls and boys;
Their faint white hands stretched out to take the toys,
And failed in taking. Childish mirth and fun
Were strangers here …
gravely they sit, anticipate no joys,
They know not who shall see tomorrow's sun!

The Rev Francis Kilvert visits his Aunt Emma at Dr Fox's private asylum at Brislington, 1874

Brislington Asylum is a fine palatial building very beautifully situated on the high ground between Keynsham and Bristol and the grounds are large and well kept. The

THE BRISTOL ROYAL HOSPITAL

FOR

SICK CHILDREN & WOMEN

ESTABLISHED 1866.

THE HOSPITAL CONTAINS 104 BEDS.

THE CONVALESCENT BRANCH AT WESTON-SUPER-MARE, 28 BEDS.

President and Hon. Treasurer: MARK WHITWILL, J.P.

Committee :

H. NAPIER ABBOT
REV. J. HARDEN CLAY, M.A.
J. CURLE, J.P. (Trades Council)
MRS. C. T. DANDO
DR. EMILY EBERLE
W. H. GREVILLE EDWARDS
MRS. W. H. GREVILLE EDWARDS
C. H. B. ELLIOTT
JONATHAN L. EVANS
HENRY FEDDEN, J.P.

WILLIAM GARNETT
MISS PHILLIPS
B. PHILLIPS (Bristol & District Teachers' Assocn.)
ALFRED N. PRICE, J.P.
DR. B. M. H. ROGERS
ALFRED J. SHORTER (Friendly Societies Council)
J. E. SMITH
E. J. SWANN, D.L., J.P.
MISS TYNDALL
REV. H. ARNOLD THOMAS, M.A.

Bankers: PRESCOTT, DIMSDALE, CAVE, TUGWELL & CO., LIMITED.
Secretary: H. LAWFORD JONES.

THE OBJECTS OF THE INSTITUTION.

1. To provide for the reception, maintenance, and medical and surgical treatment of Children under twelve years of age, in a suitable building cheerfully and salubriously placed; to furnish with advice and medicine those that cannot or need not be admitted into the Hospital; and also to receive Women suffering from diseases peculiar to their sex.
2. To promote the advancement of medical science with reference to the diseases of Women and Children, and to provide for the instruction of Students in these essential departments of medical knowledge.
3. To diffuse among all classes of the community, and particularly among the poor, a better acquaintance with the management of Infants and Children during health and sickness; and to assist in the education and training of Women in the special duties of Children's Nurses.

SPECIAL FEATURES OF THE HOSPITAL.

1. *No Note of Recommendation is required* for In- or Out-Patients, but Out-Patients pay a small fee.
2. Children under 12 years of age admitted as In-Patients—Free.
3. Women admitted on Payment—according to their means.
4. Babies of any age admitted for Medical and Surgical Treatment.
5. Special Ward for Treatment of Croup, Bronchitis, etc.
6. Four Cots for **Measles** Cases in separate Building (for children 2 to 12 years old).

CASES OF ACCIDENT AND SUDDEN ILLNESS ADMITTED AT ANY HOUR.

Annual Subscriptions and Donations are much needed, and may be sent to the Treasurer, Grove Avenue, Queen Square; or to the Secretary, at the Hospital.

TELEPHONE No. 138.

DETAILED PARTICULARS ON PAGE 761.

matron told us it was a bad day with Aunt Emma who was in unusual good health, and therefore more violent and excitable than usual. She asked us to go out into the garden to see her where she was sitting quietly, rather than bring her into the house where she might make a great noise. Aunt Emma was sitting in a low seat in a sunny corner doing some work, with a cat or two cats on her lap.

She appeared to me dingily dressed in black and she wore a hideous brown straw mushroom hat. Aunt Emma said she had been placed and was kept at Brislington by a conspiracy and by the Government who must all have their heads cut off. She was in daily danger of her life and was cursed and sworn at for a damn bitch. Mrs. Bullock and Mrs. Ford were in conspiracy against her life and Dr. Fox's Dr. Charles dared not sleep in his own house for fear of being murdered and he was obliged to sleep in the asylum every night.

Medical Men On Trial: The Clifton Convent Case

Today there was a remarkable action to recover damages against two well-known Clifton doctors, Dr H. Marshall and Dr Shaw, for negligently and improperly certifying the plaintiff Catherine Mason (35) to be insane and for libel in stating in those certificates that she was insane, and against the Mother Superior of the Benedictine Convent at Clifton Wood [Beaufort House, now demolished], Madame Gauchard, for trespass, for placing the plaintiff in temporary confinement, for slander in furnishing the doctors with evidence as to her insanity.

In the evidence it was said that she refused food, cried, slapped the Mother Superior's face, escaped from her room by letting herself down on her rug straps and threw trays of food downstairs. The doctors examined her and sent her to Dr Fox's Asylum in Brislington, and it emerged that she had a long history of mental disturbance, and the defendants were found not guilty.

Clifton Chronicle, March 1888

Joseph Lister, the pioneer of antiseptics, visits Bristol in 1889 to demonstrate his operating technique at the Museum

A woman with an abscess in her neck which required incision agreed to let the great man operate upon her, as many of us as the room would hold, including prominent citizens and a great many of the medical men of Bristol, crowded into the Museum. In the centre sat the patient, her neck swathed in the thick gauze dressing then used. She appeared very pleased with the proceedings and showed no sign of pain when Lister, after a few words of explanation, opened the abscess under the usual cloud of carbolic spray.

Wicked and cruel

I am happy to say I have never vaccinated any person and am of the opinion that such a wicked and cruel and unnatural practice should be prohibited by an Act of Parliament.

Letter from a doctor to the Clifton Chronicle, 1886

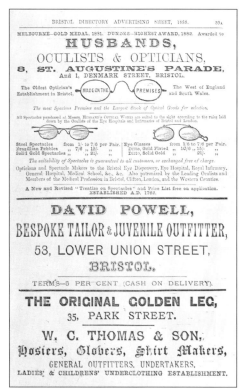

BRISTOL DIRECTORY ADVERTISING SHEET, 1888.   59a

MELBOURNE—GOLD MEDAL, 1851. DUNDEE—HIGHEST AWARD, 1882. Awarded to

HUSBANDS,
OCULISTS & OPTICIANS,
8, ST. AUGUSTINE'S PARADE,
And 1, DENMARK STREET, BRISTOL.

The Oldest Optician's   MADE ON THE   The West of England
Establishment in Bristol.   PREMISES   and South Wales.

The most Spacious Premises and the Largest Stock of Optical Goods for selection.

All Spectacles purchased at Messrs. Husbands's Optical Works are suited to the sight according to the rules laid down by the Oculists of the Eye Hospitals and Infirmaries of Bristol and London.

The suitability of Spectacles is guaranteed to all customers, or exchanged free of charge.

Steel Spectacles   from 1/- to 7/6 per Pair.   Eye Glasses   from 1/6 to 7/6 per Pair.
Brazilian Pebbles   „   7/6 „ 15/-   „   Ditto, Gold Plated   „ 10/6 „ 15/-   „
Solid Gold Spectacles   „   „ 21/-   „   Ditt'o, Solid Gold   „   21/-   „

Opticians and Spectacle Makers to the Bristol Eye Dispensary, Eye Hospital, Royal Infirmary, General Hospital, Medical School, &c., &c. Also patronised by the Leading Oculists and Members of the Medical Profession in Bristol, Clifton, London, and the Western Counties.

A New and Revised "Treatise on Spectacles" and Price List free on application.
ESTABLISHED A.D. 1762.

DAVID POWELL,
BESPOKE TAILOR & JUVENILE OUTFITTER,
53, LOWER UNION STREET,
BRISTOL.

TERMS—5 PER CENT (CASH ON DELIVERY).

THE ORIGINAL GOLDEN LEG,
35, PARK STREET.

W. C. THOMAS & SON,
Hosiers, Glovers, Shirt Makers,
GENERAL OUTFITTERS, UNDERTAKERS.
LADIES' & CHILDRENS' UNDERCLOTHING ESTABLISHMENT.

Harry Bow, professional funeral mute for Lee's, the Narrow Street undertaker, covers three funerals

I had another long busy day's work at funerals. I and father went up to Lee at 10 am, on a big contract. Four of us walks round to a house, 9, Cowley Street, Newfoundland Road. We went into a front room, sits down and had drinks round, and I had a bottle of fiz for my share. Then we took out the coffin and starts off out to Ridgeway Park. The parson wasn't on hand so we was kept waiting. I had a jaw and a lark with the other fellows and done sketches of their mugs for em, at which they was amused indeed. The parson didn't turn up so at last we carried it down and our conductor reads the service over instead.

All being over we mounts up and rattles off at a fine pace back into town and starts off to do another job in Clark Street. We went in and the others had drinks again, me nought. We took the coffin along the Cut to Bath Bridge and Arno's Vale and puts it away all right, then rides out at a fast pace back into town. There was still another job in Milk Street, for Arno's Vale and for the third time today I shoulders the coffin. We took it in down a steep awkward place and then we found the grave was not ready yet, and had to stand and wait while the two sextons works to finish it. Then we puts it in all right, joyfully retires, strips off our plumes, got aboard and amid talk and chaff, rides back into town to the shop and unloads. The boss pays I hard earned rhino, 3 shillings, so thats good biz and the way to scoop em, and we had quite a big field day of it for 7 hours at a stretch and done a lot of walks and riding about indeed. Good iron.

Henry Bow's Diary, February 2nd, 1893

The Plague (typhoid) at Clifton, 1897

The air here is full of sorrow. In two families we know there have been deaths, one a dear little boy of eight and his brother is lying in a most critical condition; in the other a charming girl, the only daughter. The children in my house are all quite convalescent, for which we are most thankful. We hope the plague is stayed but in the College many boys and three masters are all very ill … I have been so worried and anxious.

Letter from novelist Emma Marshall, 26 Sion Hill

Sweet Tooth writes to the *Clifton Chronicle* in July 1899

The belief that sugar ruins the teeth of children is utterly groundless, seeing that the finest, whitest and strongest teeth are found in the mouths of negroes brought up in sugar plantations, who from their earliest years upwards consume more sugar than any other class of people whatever.

George Muller's funeral, March 14, 1898

The funeral will long be remembered by all those who witnessed it as a most remarkable exhibition of popular regard and affection. It was all the more remarkable inasmuch as he had never associated himself with the people in their social or civic life. Tens of thousands of persons lined the route through which the funeral procession passed. One most gratifying feature was the very large proportion of the working classes who turned out to pay their last tribute of respect. Nothing like it had ever been seen in Bristol before. In all the leading thoroughfares black shutters were put up, or blinds drawn; flags were at half mast on Bristol Cathedral and other churches; and muffled peals were rung. The whole city may be said to have been in mourning.

Outside the Bethesda Chapel – in fact all along the remaining line of route – an immense concourse of people had gathered. The carriages also were supplemented by numerous fresh arrivals, including the Mayor's state coach. It is estimated that over eighty carriages joined into the procession to the cemetery (Arno's Vale). The vast body of people was the more to be noticed from the fact that the funeral arrangements were characterised by the utmost simplicity – there was an entire absence of any attempt at show. The demonstrations, quiet, reverent, and sympathetic, from the crowds en route was a really remarkable ending to a remarkable career.

From Arno's Vale Cemetery – a sonnet by H.D. Rawnsley, 1877

Here let me walk a little while in peace!
Ye dead, stretch out your quiet hands to me!
For here, the merchant from his traffic free,
Nor feels his failure, nor his goods' increase;
The shopman here, of counter-worries cease;
The sailor quite forgets how roared the sea;
No lawyer rates his client for a fee;
And all the City's wounded ones have ease!

Demure middle-class church-going in the 1880s.

10 – The See of Faith

On a bright cold morning in October, 1881, people in Bristol went to church and chapel as usual. But unbeknown to them, the *Western Daily Press* had organised a religious census.

The public had not been told so that the returns would represent average attendance; each minister was given a form and asked to see that it was filled in by someone in authority. Altogether 198 congregations of 30 denominations were counted, and it was found that an astounding (to us) 109,452 adults had attended a service.

As expected the largest attendance was by members of the Church of England, 45,518 of them, followed by the Congregationalists. 3,342 went to Roman Catholic services. The best individual attendance was at St Paul's, Bedminster where 2,316 turned up. There were 147 worshippers at Horfield prison, the Salvation Army attracted 1,291 members and the Temperance Army 406. This was the third religious census in the city over 40 years, and every time, Bristol figures were higher than for other industrial cities of equivalent size. Religion was a major part of the glue that kept Victorian society functioning. It was a fact of life: every school had a daily religious service, grand homes held prayers for family and servants, big employers held daily prayers, and the majority of children went to Sunday School.

Church and chapel provided many of the things the welfare state provides now. For the poor, it was a lifeline, providing warmth, company, food, and instruction, and escape from cramped sub-standard homes. The churches and chapels ran schools and Sunday schools, libraries, choirs, evening classes. They paid for medical care, they opened working men's clubs, organised sports, they put on plays, held spelling bees, Bible classes, housewifery classes, lectures, outings. Religion was regarded as an instrument for bringing about social change, and improving behaviour – and it worked, notably with education, and through the temperance movement.

Social life for the working and middle class revolved around the church or chapel, with the better-off working all year round making 'comforts' for the poor, by running bazaars and fêtes and sales of work; the church gave occupation to idle affluent middle-class ladies who knitted and sewed and made objets d'art to sell to raise money to help the less well-off. In fact the middle classes believed that the civilising effect of religion was one of the reasons why the British masses had never risen up in riot or revolution, and saw charity and good works as their particular contribution.

It was a good system, so far as regular church-goers were concerned, but the welfare handouts were rarely extended to non-believers; help went to the grateful and deserving church-goers, not the undeserving heathen, and the people who decided which category supplicants belonged to were the middle classes. The rich churches and chapels ran missions in the poor areas, but only reached those who attended regularly. So the very worst poverty and need was not met, except by the Quakers and the Salvation Army, both of which set up missions in the city in 1880.

A Quaker missionary, C.R. Parsons, who worked for the City Mission in a poor district wrote of his work:

> To be brought into contact with so much strife, and wretchedness and vice – to see so much poverty and misery he cannot relieve; to hear on all hands loud complaints against Providence and hard sayings against God; to stand in the midst of contagion and disease, to see the profound indifference of vast masses of people to their present and future well-being; to witness harrowing scenes of terrible death beds, more or less depresses the soul and exhausts the whole man.

Nor was it all sweetness and light in the churches themselves. Bristol was not always a tolerant city; when the Catholic Emancipation Bill was being proposed, some 20,000 Bristolians held a meeting in Queen Square to protest, and the city had been famous in the seventeenth century for persecuting dissenters.

By Victoria's reign, the Bristol non-conformists were accepted and indeed in total outnumbered the Anglicans; they sat on the Conservative city council, welcome because they were major employers in the city and great philanthropists. But anti-Catholic and to a lesser extent, anti-Jewish feeling, ran high, fermented by letters and articles in the local press. And in the Church of England itself, there was a vicious rift between the evangelical Low and the ritualistic High Anglicans from the 1840s onwards, this too stemming from the distrust of 'Popery'.

The Anglican church in Bristol also felt aggrieved at its loss of status, for in 1837, the diocese of Bristol was united with Gloucester, leaving the city, they said, with 'half a Bishop and half a cathedral', and neither was remedied until the 1880s, when Bristol got its Bishopric back, and the nave of the Cathedral was completed.

There were absurd rows over church architecture because of the fear and distrust of Papists; when the Pro-Cathedral was built in Park Place in 1850, there was an outcry about the statues designed for the porch, and lectures at the Victoria Rooms on topics like 'Papal aggression'.

The installation of the first Catholic Bishop in Bristol in 1850 caused a furore. Sermons against Papal intrusion were preached in the Anglican churches, and effigies were burned on Brandon Hill. There was similar uproar at Bristol Cathedral in 1876 when new statues of the Virgin Mary, and four saints, one wearing a papal tiara, another a cardinal's hat, had to be removed from the porch, after virulent protests in the local press about the creeping influence of Catholicism, and the insult to Protestantism. It was not

St Mary Redcliffe before the spire was reinstated.

St Matthew's Kingsdown, designed by Thomas Rickman and built in the 1830s, was one of an astonishing number of 44 Anglican churches built in the city in the nineteenth century. [J. Jones, engraved 1854; courtesy Bristol Museums and Art Gallery]

a coincidence that the statue of the Virgin was smashed in the process of removal.

In fact Roman Catholics were well established by the 1850s, with an estimated 2,000 living in the city. Numbers grew partly because Clifton was regarded as a retirement resort, and attracted a number of Catholic in-comers, and partly because many Irish immigrants settled after being employed to work on the railways and the docks. By 1843 they acquired St Mary on the Quay and a decade later there were two Catholic convents, one at Arno's Court and one at Westbury-on-Trym; by the end of the century there were another three churches and another five small convents.

When St Mary's opened, the *Bristol Journal* thundered a warning to Protestant readers not to be betrayed into departure from their faith 'by the gorgeous ceremonies, the fascinating music and above all the gentle aspect it wears in Protestant England. Here it puts forth only velvet claws; history tells us how deadly is its clutch.'

Anglicans saw it as their duty to convert the Catholics and formed the Bristol Protestant Association for the purpose of 'disseminating knowledge of the principles and practices of the church of Rome', and aimed at the Jews, whose first synagogue opened in Temple Street in 1842, was the Society for the Promotion of Christianity among the Jews. Jews were tolerated by the business community and by the Protestants because they made no attempt to proselytise, and so had their first city councillors elected by 1850. Catholics had to wait much longer.

The Bristol Protestants were proselytisers, they ran societies like the one 'to promote the moral and religious improvement of the Irish', there was a Domestic Mission 'for visiting the poor in their habitations and affording them temporal and spiritual aid'. There was even one for the Liberation of Religion from State Patronage, as well as a mission to the Turks, and a mission whose aim was to visit 'the 70,000 or 80,000 people in the city who systematically absent themselves from the public means of grace', and sought to 'present the plan of salvation before the ignorant, the careless and the depraved'.

But while religious tolerance and a spirit of liberalism gradually extended to every other denomination, the Anglicans themselves were at war, Low church against High church. The growth of the Oxford Movement, which called for a return to the old rituals, with a romantic harking back to the medieval use of vestments, raised chancels, a reredos (St John's in Bedminster was the first church in the country to have one since the Reformation), incense, sung Eucharist, and the abolition of pews and galleries. To the evangelical wing, this was 'the foolery of Rome'. They wanted plain services, no dressing up and no fancy church furniture.

As the movement grew, a few churches 'went over', and new ones were built; the hotbeds of ritualism were notably All Saints in Clifton, St Raphael's in Cumberland Road, Holy Trinity, Horfield, St Mark's in Easton, St John's in Bedminster, and Holy Nativity, Knowle. Crowds came, attracted by the light and colour and richness of the furnishings, and the drama of the ritual, after the drab Evangelical services they were used to.

Tracts and counter-tracts were distributed, controversy raged in the newspapers and the Bishop was frequently asked to intervene, when Anglican churches had the nerve to put up the Stations of the Cross, a canopy over the altar, or to hold processions led by a crucifix.

The complaints frequently came from Clifton. On the whole the richer you were, generally the plainer you liked your churches. Parishioners of Christchurch complained to the Bishop that at All Saints, candles were used for show, not lighting, that the clergy turned their backs on the congregation during Communion and wore 'a garment known as a maniple', and that the congregation made the sign of the cross, and bowed.

The power of the churchmen also led to theological confrontations, like the one in 1876 between the Rev. Flavel Cook, vicar of Christchurch, Clifton, and one of his congregation, Henry Jenkins, over an obscure theological point in a book he had written. Cook denied Jenkins communion, and the case went to court and ran for days, with coverage in the national press. The *Clifton Chronicle* put on an extra 1,000 copies on the day the verdict was announced. Cook lost, expensively, and had to resign. Religion mattered deeply to Victorian Bristolians.

This surge of religious feeling led to a remarkable growth in the number of new churches – many of them now demolished or being used for other purposes. Forty-four new Anglican churches alone were built, the majority paid for by public subscription, plus diocesan grants, and this was matched by the number of new chapels and missions built by the non-conformists.

Between 1850 and 1919 the number of places of worship in the city rose from 83 to 260.

As well as making a huge contribution to the welfare of the citizens of Bristol, they altered the architectural landscape of the city, with results that we can still see today, in an age when all denominations struggle with dwindling congregations and decaying buildings. The Victorian age in Bristol was indeed an age of faith.

Snapshots of Religion

Church discipline

Z.A. having attended a late week evening service in a state of intoxication, but having expressed great penitence, and the Church being satisfied from evidence adduced that his general conduct is good, it was resolved that he be suspended from Communion for two months.

Mr Wood having informed the church that Y.B. was convicted at the Quarter Sessions of stealing, and sentenced to three months' imprisonment, it was resolved that he be expelled from Communion with the Church, with the earnest desire and prayer of its members that he may be brought to a speedy and sincere repentance. Expelled W.D. for dishonourable conduct in business. Suspended for a month.

X.C. having fallen into the habit of intemperance, it was resolved that he be suspended from Communion with this church for the present. [Three years afterwards it appeared that X.C. had repented of his sin and displayed the genuineness of his repentance by upwards of two years' sobriety and good conduct, whereupon it was resolved that X.C. be restored to Communion.]

From the minute books of Zion Congregational Church, Bedminster, 1843-50

The undeserving poor

Along the straight line of streets which lead to the District Church of Holy Trinity (St. Philips) from the centre of the city, I met with a diversity of persons, but many of them affording too little cause of congratulation either to society or themselves. Here the unwashed operative, with a beard of a week's growth, and luxuriating in the unshaved and untended laziness of an idle morning, loitered about with his face turned far oftener in the direction of a public house than the parish Church, and looking still more repulsive in the filthy contrast he presented to the thrifty and tidily dressed artisan, of his own trade perhaps, and probably with no more than his own means, bound, in company with his wife and child, to a place of worship. Then by angles, for the most part adjoining beerhouses on which the sun shone, basked and smoked indolent, heavy-handed, bulkish men in smock frocks, who though they had apparently washed their faces, were in other respects brutalised as men could be – coarse in speech and besotted in mind.

The Churchgoer, Joseph Leech, 1844

The power of prayer

This morning I had only one farthing left, like the handful of meal in the barrel, when on my usual walk before breakfast I felt myself led out of my usual track into a direction in

St Jude's the Dings, designed by S.B. Gabriel, 1849.

which I had not gone for some months. In stepping over a stile I said to myself 'perhaps God has a reason even in this.' About five minutes afterwards I met a Christian gentleman who gave me two sovereigns for the Orphans, and then I knew the reason why I had been led this way.

George Muller's Journal, February 2nd, 1844

A Sunday School outing of the Old King Street Baptist Sunday School, 1868

A very general desire having been expressed to vary the anniversary services by an excursion in preference to the usual tea meeting, the children were taken in covered vans to a field lent for the purpose by Mr Greenway of Hambrook. The day was beautifully fine and both before and after tea the children with their teachers amused themselves with various games. At the close prizes were awarded to the successful competitors and after singing a hymn for Mr Greenway the children re-entered the vans and were driven home, no mishaps having occurred to mar the pleasure of the day. [The outing the following year was to New Passage by train, and a Punch and Judy show was provided.]

Intolerance

I was walking down Richmond Hill when I was accosted by a young gentleman attired in the ultra-ritualistic clerical garb who inquired directions for All Saints Church. I told him and explained the route and he then asked if I could tell him at what hour 'mass' commenced. I made no comment!

Clifton Chronicle, 1850

Wolves in sheep's clothing

Sir, Yesterday on my return home over Durdham Down my attention was suddenly attracted by two persons, the one a youth about 18 years of age, the other a priest or Jesuit habited in the usual garb of that class of evil spirits now prowling about all over England, like wolves in sheep's clothing, seeking whom they can devour.

St Thomas's Eastville, designed by H.C.M. Hirst and consecrated in 1889.

In passing me, I heard the ghostly man exclaim in a foreign accent: 'They are the enemies of God and man.' The Jesuit or priest had placed his fangs in an excited manner on the youth, who appeared rather desirous of disengaging himself from the grasp of the unwelcome expounder of the religious opinion which he sought to inculcate. In this way he continued his denunciations, calculated to frighten the youth into an acquiescence in his doctrines, in the style of a highwayman propounding his alternatives; your purse or your life. Turn Roman Catholic or prepare for eternal perdition.

Letter from Disgusted of Clifton, to the Bristol Times, 1852

Elopement of a Jewess, 1858

Miss Gertrude Isaacs of Pritchard Street quitted the maternal roof for the purpose of executing some commission in the city for her mother, by whom her return was for several hours anxiously expected. Nothing transpired… until 2 o'clock when a note was received from her stating that at nine o'clock she had been united in wedlock to Mr Taylor, asking for forgiveness and assigning no reason why she had acted in so clandestine a manner, convinced that her parents and friends would never have given consent to the match.

For our own part we are induced to regard it from a more cheering point of view and to note in it another sign of the growing disposition of the age to overleap those religious sectarian barricades which have too long divided the members of the common human family.

Editorial comment in the Bristol Mercury, 1858

A church for the rich

It is not the church of a poor man, he has no business there, in that atmosphere of eau de cologne, bouquet de la reine, where the glitters of gilt-edged prayer books and the rustle of brocades present sounds and sights extraordinary to humble comprehension. Dowagers young and old, all finely clad, nodding plumes and flowing dresses swept on and still the expectants stood by the porch, for the free seats had been taken by powdered footmen.

John Leech, alias *The Churchgoer*, on St Andrew's, Clifton in the 1850s. The church rented out pews to those who could afford them.

The 1860 restoration of Bristol Cathedral

The pattern and materials are such as would disgrace a railway station or the showroom of a cheap lath and plaster warehouse.

Ecclesiologist, Bristol Journal

A deathbed scene

When the leaves began to fall, Jim visibly declined and Max knew that the feet of this child, whom God has sent him, would soon touch the waters of the dark river. But there was light beyond for Dandy Jim. His mother was there at the last; and Robin hushed his sobs; and Matt Ford and Dick Willing stood by with folded arms and faces of suppressed emotion, watching the flickering of the little life so soon to be extinguished here, to shine for ever in the Paradise of God.

'Max, dear Max!' the child said. 'Goodnight, I'm going home, Max! God bless you, Max!' Then suddenly: 'Mother, I see our baby! She is so pretty! And there's heaps of flowers! Look, mother, look!'

But Jim's eyes saw what other eyes saw not; and then with one bright smile, he cried exultingly: 'I see Jesus too!' And Jim was in the presence of the Lord of Love and Grace.

From Dandy Jim, the Bristol Newspaper Boy, by Emma Marshall, c.1860

A Sunday School scholar comes back to Old King Street Baptist Church, 1866

The school was addressed by – Broad, who stated that he had lived a somewhat irregular life, and had been in three regiments. The teaching of his Sunday school days had not however been lost. Often in his revelry had he thought of what he had been taught there, and he believed it was mainly owing to these recollections that he had been led to see the error of his ways and become a changed character. He hoped he had come home to do some good to those around him; this at least was his desire and he hoped that through God's blessing he should be able to succeed.

Danger in church

Had the man in the bowler and smock frock who appeared in the pulpit on Sunday evening and alarmed the congregation [of Trinity Church, Hotwells] just assembled not been a harmless lunatic but a rough bent on mischief, a terrified and crowded congregation could not possibly escape from the church however they might try, and the consequences are fearful to contemplate.
Letter to the Western Daily Press, 1874

Clifton College Mission at St Barnabas, Ashley Road, 1875

Muck-heaps and farm refuse, on which jerry builders had set up rows of houses, which periodically got flooded and sucked up fever and death from chill for poor folk who lived there. No lamps, streets only wadeable through. A few public houses of the worst sort.
The Rev H.D. Rawnsley's description of his parish

A Sunday School Treat for Redfield Wesleyan Chapel, 1880s

The venue for many years was Farmer Veale's farm, and the programme for this red letter day in our Sunday School Life was usually as follows: the first duty of the teachers and officers was to attend a prayer meeting at 6am, there to ask for fine weather, and for the protection against harm and accident for all those taking part in the day's festivities.

After this the various members of staff proceeded to cut up bread and butter and cake, while others packed a portion of each in paper bags, each bag containing sufficient food for a scholar. Others assisted in loading vans with seats for the accommodation of adult visitors, tables, urns for preparing tea, the aforesaid bags of food, ginger beer, sweets and all the other necessities for assured comfort and enjoyment of the children, their parents and friends. At about 11am the children and their teachers formed in class around the Chapel and at a given signal proceeded in order of seniority to the river bank at Crew's Hole, where barges were waiting to transport them to the farm on the other side. A senior scholar carried the school banner at the head of the procession. The voyage across the river was naturally very short, but sufficient time was always found for the singing of the nautical hymn 'We are out upon the ocean sailing'.

Advice to Girls in the *Girl's Own Paper* 1891

Dorothy: If you wish to do good service, over and above your family and natural duties at home, we suggest that you can procure packets of nice little books (tracts) and the Holy Gospels, from our publishing office, and when you travel by land or water, or even take a drive in any hired vehicle, you can leave them to be found – under a seat cushion, for remember that many of the lower orders feel insulted by the offer of one – a result of which you should beware, so as not to defeat your own object.

Religion and alcohol

At Highbury Chapel in Redland in the 1890s there was 'a divergence of opinion over wine used at Communion. Some said it should be alcoholic, others were unable to agree, so they had to compromise and have alcohol in the morning, and non-alcohol in the evening so people could choose which service to attend.'

Keep Sunday Special

At the Police Court on Thursday nine lads aged 15–18 were charged with playing cards at the Hotwells on a Sunday afternoon. There had been complaints in the neighbourhood. Fined 1s. 6d. each or two days imprisonment.

Bristol Observer, 1897

SIXTY FOUR YEARS
1837-1901
A QUEEN

QUEEN VICTORIA
Born 24ᵗʰ May 1819 · Crowned 27ᵗʰ June 1838
Died 22ⁿᵈ Jan 1901 in the 64ᵗʰ Year

Hats, Caps, Shirts,

Hosiery,

Gloves, Umbrellas, &c.

W. F. WINTER.
The Up-to-Date Clothier, Hatter, Hosier & Tailor,
58, High St. & 162, Snargate St.,
DOVER.

Bespoke Tailoring.

Suits, to Measure,
from 21/-.

Trousers - - from 6/6.

11 – Epilogue: 1901

BY JANUARY 1901, WHEN QUEEN VICTORIA DIED, Bristol was recognisable as the modern city we know today.

The Victorian road, rail and tram systems that are the basis of today's transport infrastructure were in place, with seven railway stations, trams covering 14 routes, an omnibus service to the further suburbs, and 35 stands for hackney carriages. Steamers and steamship companies could take Bristolians to 70 destinations worldwide.

The city's administration, the composition of the city council, the judicial system, were essentially those we have today. Water and sewage systems had been laid out, there was a municipal refuse collection, the city had charge of the police force, the central police and fire stations had been set up at Bridewell, and Horfield Gaol had been built. Reluctantly, because the rate-payers objected, the Corporation was beginning to build council housing.

The financial heart of the city had been established, with a stock exchange, 10 banks, 60 insurance companies, 18 building societies. The street directory for 1901 listed a page of accountants, and 270 barristers and solicitors. The industrial city was still concentrated on the central area, and was still a significant part of the city's economy.

Great strides had been made in public health, and 210 physicians and surgeons were now practising. Mortality rates had been reduced thanks to better sanitation, slum housing was gradually being demolished, and infant mortality went down to 16 deaths per thousand.

There had been enormous progress: in the 64 years of Victoria's reign, Bristolians had seen the arrival of a postal system, telegrams, the telephone, the typewriter, compulsory education, public transport, photography, the bicycle, the first motor car, moving pictures. The technological developments of the Victorian age were dazzling, and thanks to Brunel, Bristol had for some of the time been at the leading edge.

Some aspects of Bristol in 1901 would be less recognisable. The City Docks still played a major role in city life, and the Centre was still home to shipping, but in the national league, the port had declined from second most important in the country to tenth. This was the year when the Avonmouth Docks Extension Scheme was given the Royal Assent. Shipbuilding was prospering.

Bristol was still essentially a manufacturing city; a breakdown of employment by trades shows 6.2 per cent working in food and drink, 7.3 in shops, 3 per cent in mechanical engineering, 14 per cent in footwear, 4.1 in paper and printing, and 7.8 in construction. Christopher Thomas, in the building that now houses Gardiners, in Broad Plain, was making eight per cent of the soap produced in Britain. Industries now virtually vanished, like boot and shoe making, pottery and ironfounding, were at their peak, and selling their goods nationally, as were Wills and Fry's, who went from 193 employees in the mid-century to 5,000 in 1901.

Bristol still had seven coalfields, though they had shrunk to producing only one per cent of the national output. Some Victorian industries had gone, notably glass, sugar, and brass and copper.

The 1901 city was smaller than now in terms of geographical size, for Shirehampton and Westbury-on-Trym and part of Henbury and Horfield were not yet inside the city boundary, but the population was higher – the 1901 census counted 328,844 inhabitants living in 54,412 dwellings. By then, 80 per cent of Britons lived in cities, and Bristol's housing stock had grown enormously – and there had been 23 streets named after the monarch. The rateable value of the city had climbed from £406,206 in 1841 to £1,561,891.

1901 was the year when the Bristol Tramways staff who expressed dissatisfaction with their working conditions were dismissed, and on union advice, 450 workers handed in their notice. The company recruited new drivers and the dissidents were never re-employed, despite complaints that the new drivers were causing accidents. By 1901, trade union membership was high, with over 100 trade and labour organisations active, and 59 trade unions, including one for women. Muller's orphanages were full, and there were three workhouses.

It was also the year when the Salvation Army, who provided a roof for some 5,000 'sleepers' a year, felt the need to set up a women's hostel for 40 to 50 females, who had to pay 3d. a night. If they worked in the laundry, they stayed free. A municipal lodging house for men had been opened by the council, and these refuges were needed for in 1901, 30 per cent of the population lived below the poverty line. So of Bristol's 1901 population, it can be estimated that at least 100,000 lived in poverty.

Bristolians were by now largely literate, thanks to the 1870 Education Act, which brought in compulsory education to the age of 13. In 1850 scarcely half the population could sign their names, but by 1900 only 3 per cent had to sign with a cross. The city had its own university college, founded in 1876.

Private schools established in Victoria's reign and still going strong are Clifton College, Clifton High School, Colston's Girls and Redland High School; there were also 65 boarding schools for young ladies and 20 for gentlemen. Run by the city or the churches were 47 Board schools and 43 National and British schools, as well as seven industrial and reform schools. Charities ran nine endowed schools. It was estimated that the crime rate fell thanks to compulsory education, for there were thousands fewer children on the streets as truancy rates went down; in 1873 school attendance was only 70 per cent of children of school age, but by 1901, 85 per cent were attending.

A very sedate College Green. Victoria's statue has since moved a little nearer the Centre.

The Victorians were church-goers, and by now over 300 clergymen and ministers are listed in *Wright's Directory*, ministering at well over 500 chapels and churches.

Charitable organisations and benevolent societies abounded in 1901: for Hopeful Discharged Females, the Club for Poor Women, the Blanket Lending Society, the Emigration Society, the Guild of Poor Things, the Depot for Ladies of Limited Means, the Temperance House for Fallen Women, the Magic Lantern Mission, as well as the more familiar Band of Hope and the Boys Brigade, and still in existence are the (R)SPCA, the SPCK, and the NSPCC. There were 20 almshouses, and 11 Temperance societies.

In terms of shopping, Bristol had 54 fishmongers, hundreds of greengrocers, butchers, grocers and bakers, 100 or more dining rooms, 32 restaurants, five department stores, 37 hotels and 16 temperance hotels, over 200 hairdressers, 50 pawnbrokers, and over 400 pubs. People still shopped regularly at markets, at St Nicholas, at Union Street, and at the daily cheese and fish markets. By 1901 Castle Street, demolished in the Blitz, had almost 100 businesses trading.

As for the cultural life of the city, there were 22 music societies, four music halls, two theatres, a city art gallery and museum, eight public libraries, 61 booksellers and seven daily and weekly newspapers, of which the *Western Daily Press* and the *Bristol Observer* still survive. But Bristol lagged behind in civic pride: the other great trading cities, Birmingham, Manchester, Liverpool and Leeds had built their libraries, museums and art galleries much earlier than Bristol, which never even built a Town Hall. Citizens could watch 'living moving pictures' at two music halls, the two theatres, the Colston Hall and the Victoria Rooms.

The year had opened sadly with the death of the Queen, and as the *Clifton Chronicle* reported, in a newspaper printed with black borders, 'signs of mourning were universal, with every social function abandoned and numerous events postponed.' Churches were draped in black, and were packed with big congregations all dressed in deep mourning. Shop window displays were funereal, and on the day of the funeral, February 2nd, the city came to a halt, transport stopped, and wreaths were placed on the Queen's statue on College Green. Muffled bells were rung, and nearly everyone on the street was dressed in black. Photographs of floral tributes sent to Windsor by Clifton College and University College were put on display.

But once the funeral was over, there was a sense that with a new King, things would change, that with a new century, a new modern era was about to dawn. The Bristol Rifles and Gloucester Volunteers had just returned from fighting in the Boer War, the end of which was in sight, and Bristol was confident and prosperous. It was to be a new dawn – if not quite the one that Victorian Bristolians expected.

Snapshots of 1901

Poem on the death of the Queen by Rose Lilian Williams of Clifton
A wail of sorrow and a burst of song,
And then a silence tender as a tear,
leave her, lov'd Queen, to her cherished rest.

Progress
Bristol's crowded thoroughfares teeming with life and activity; its busy marts of commerce, extensive manufactories, handsome public buildings and streets; its civic, educational, commercial, scientific, religious and philanthropic institutions; its rapid increase in population, both in the city and in the environs, its sanitary improvements, its extension of docks and railways, its unique system of electric tramways, its erection of new and restoration of old churches, its superb arrangements for electric light and its magnificent suburbs, public recreation grounds and palatial residences of merchants, manufacturers, traders and others, all point to the fact that the city and port of Bristol has made rapid strides and is fully alive to the competition of modern times, and that

the place still retains its ancient prestige as one of the most important centres of the kingdom.

Arrowsmith's Dictionary of Bristol

Housing the poor

There are still in Bristol a deplorable number of slums where houses are crowded together in a very undesirable way. It would be a revelation to some of the dwellers in the residential districts of the West and North to be shown the many various courts of Redcliffe and Bedminster, St Philips, St James's and St Augustine, St Michael's and Hotwells. The manner in which houses were squeezed into the narrowest space by a former generation of builders is indeed remarkable.

The Health Committee have not seen their way to take drastic action that some desired. The difficulties and costliness of dealing with slums is proverbial; but from time to time houses have been declared unfit for habitation and thus many of the worst of the buildings have been condemned. In this quiet way since 1890, 339 of the most undesirable dwellings were closed by civic intervention and 182 made habitable by repairs and alteration. A number of small dwellings has been built by the Corporation to re-house people who have been dispossessed by the demolition of their former residences by improvement schemes, but the new buildings have proved costly and the result has not escaped criticism.

Bristol As it Was And Is

Education for girls

The latter half of the nineteenth century produced a remarkable change in the general attitude in regard to the education of girls and the place of women in some of the activities of the busy world. Our great-grandparents would certainly be astonished at the great stream of girls and young women leaving the factories after their day's work [which] would afford material for many questions as to how it came about that so much of the industrial work of the city was being done by women. Equally surprised would they be if at some of the highest scholastic institutions they found many girls, not engaged in plain sewing, sampler decoration or even the etceteras of a finishing academy, but in experiments with ill-smelling chemicals, with problems of physics and other studies involved in preparation for the BSc. degree. Whether these tendencies are wholly for good, or whether there is a danger of carrying them to an extreme must be left for others to discuss.

Bristol As it Was And Is

The rebuilt Colston Hall opens, 1900

Although everyone regretted the destruction of a hall, the interior architecture of which had much that commended it, [it is] a larger and more convenient and safer building. The courageous policy of the Colston Hall Company has resulted in effecting a great improvement upon older conditions. The hall has seating accommodation for 3,560 and the total can be increased by using standing space, thus bringing up the accommodation to 5,000. The Lesser hall seats 600, and the premises include several other rooms used for public gatherings.

The relief of Mafeking

The Rev W.H. Weekes, an Old Boy, was in Mafeking throughout the seven months' siege, and came to Prize Day at his old school. He arrived by train at Clifton Down Station and was greeted by fog-signals, by the headmaster and a great number of the boys. Flags were placed on the carriage which was awaiting him, the horses were taken from the shafts, and to the accompaniment of trumpets, whistles and cheers, with cyclists forming an unofficial guard of honour, the boys drew him home in triumph.
C.P. Hill, History of Bristol Grammar School

The Thomas Edison Picture show at the Colston Hall in October 1901

… showed a snippet of cricket, with Mold bowling to A.H. Hornby, a lion tamer in action and a half-hour story of a Newfoundland fishing trip containing three miles of film. It was almost too much for the Colston Hall. Its electrical facilities proved inadequate and Thomas Edison had to delay the first performance while it installed a dynamo. Even then the bulky machine blew a couple of fuses. But such minor technical hitches did not stop 140,000 admissions in the first four weeks of a six week stay.
A City and its Cinemas

Winston Churchill at the Victoria Rooms, 1900

Mr Churchill talked about his experiences as a reporter during the Boer War, his capture and escape, and spoke in an easy colloquial style with the fluency of one who speaks from his own experiences and the audience hung almost breathless on his words.
Western Daily Press

The Co-op decides to start window dressing, 1901

The logic of Co-operative shopkeeping is, of course, opposed to this system, and the Committee are quite naturally reluctant to expose goods to the risk of deterioration by using them for the mere purposes of display. But with proper safeguards this risk may be reduced to a minimum, and Co-operators have everything to gain from the exhibition of their own wares, 'hall-marked' as they are by a guarantee that the labour expended upon their production and distribution has been carefully regarded and that they represent the highest standard of purity and excellence to the consumer.
Industrial Democracy in Bristol

Clara Butt marries Kennerley Rumford in Bristol Cathedral, June 26th, 1900

Bristolians had the day off and it seemed the entire city turned out to honour her. Special trains from London were laid on, church bells were rung, and the city presented her with a diamond brooch, made in initials CB, Clara Butt or City of Bristol, transfixed with a ruby arrow.

There was a minor riot when the cathedral opened to fill up the remaining places after the 500 official guests had been allowed in; among them were Madame Albani, Belle

Cole, Nellie Melba, and Forbes Robertson, and many other well-known singers sat in the choir stalls and joined in the hymns. Sir Arthur Sullivan, who was to have played the organ, but was ill, had composed a special Wedding Anthem, *O God Thou Art Worthy To Be Praised*.

Clara wore a dress in heavy cream crepe de chine trimmed with a silk fringe and her sisters were bridesmaids. The Queen sent her a wedding present.

The Best In The Kingdom

Horse-drawn trams have virtually disappeared in Bristol, and we now have an excellent service of electric trams – the most up-to-date in the Kingdom, including London. The extended Hotwells section was opened last Thursday and residents who patronised the service were delighted with the comfort, space, lighting and speed of the trams which furnish luxurious riding. The cars are 30 feet long and accommodate 24 people inside and 29 people outside, the upper deck being fitted with rainproof seats. Inside each car is handsomely fitted up, the ceilings being of birdseye maple enriched with walnut mouldings, and the seats tastefully upholstered in velvet cushions. Incandescent lamps furnish ample light at night and electric buttons are at hand in all parts of the car for signalling it to stop. Passengers can travel four and a half miles for three pence, with intermediate penny sections in proportion.

Bristol Observer, December 1900

Clifton High School mourns Queen Victoria

A picture remains in my mind of the whole School, even the smallest children, dressed in unrelieved black, for the state of public feeling at that time demanded this form of expression of the universality of mourning for the great Queen.

Catherine Burns, headmistress 1891-1908

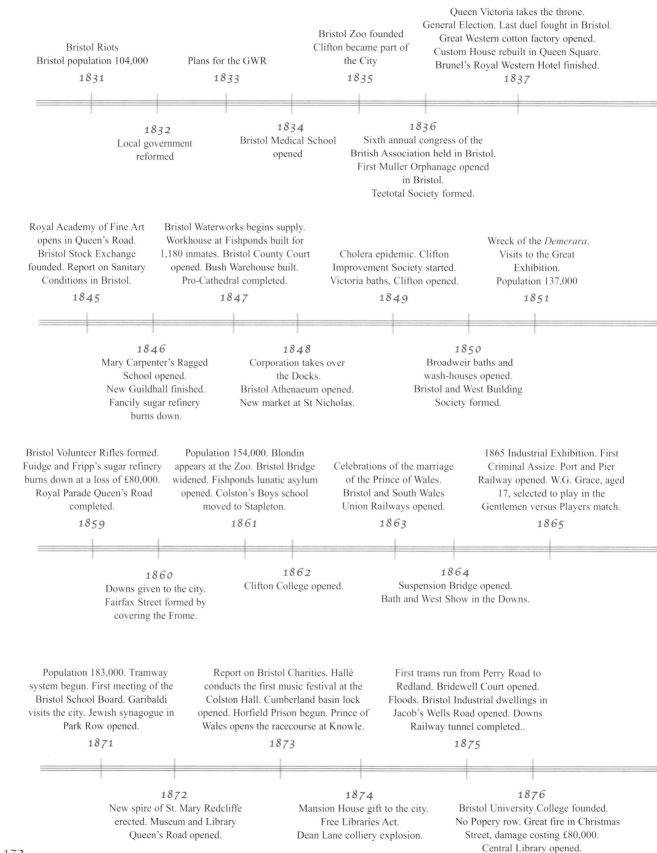

Bristol Riots
Bristol population 104,000
1831

Plans for the GWR
1833

Bristol Zoo founded
Clifton became part of
the City
1835

Queen Victoria takes the throne.
General Election. Last duel fought in Bristol.
Great Western cotton factory opened.
Custom House rebuilt in Queen Square.
Brunel's Royal Western Hotel finished.
1837

1832
Local government
reformed

1834
Bristol Medical School
opened

1836
Sixth annual congress of the
British Association held in Bristol.
First Muller Orphanage opened
in Bristol.
Teetotal Society formed.

Royal Academy of Fine Art
opens in Queen's Road.
Bristol Stock Exchange
founded. Report on Sanitary
Conditions in Bristol.
1845

Bristol Waterworks begins supply.
Workhouse at Fishponds built for
1,180 inmates. Bristol County Court
opened. Bush Warehouse built.
Pro-Cathedral completed.
1847

Cholera epidemic. Clifton
Improvement Society started.
Victoria baths, Clifton opened.
1849

Wreck of the *Demerara*.
Visits to the Great
Exhibition.
Population 137,000
1851

1846
Mary Carpenter's Ragged
School opened.
New Guildhall finished.
Fancily sugar refinery
burns down.

1848
Corporation takes over
the Docks.
Bristol Athenaeum opened.
New market at St Nicholas.

1850
Broadweir baths and
wash-houses opened.
Bristol and West Building
Society formed.

Bristol Volunteer Rifles formed.
Fuidge and Fripp's sugar refinery
burns down at a loss of £80,000.
Royal Parade Queen's Road
completed.
1859

Population 154,000. Blondin
appears at the Zoo. Bristol Bridge
widened. Fishponds lunatic asylum
opened. Colston's Boys school
moved to Stapleton.
1861

Celebrations of the marriage
of the Prince of Wales.
Bristol and South Wales
Union Railways opened.
1863

1865 Industrial Exhibition. First
Criminal Assize. Port and Pier
Railway opened. W.G. Grace, aged
17, selected to play in the
Gentlemen versus Players match.
1865

1860
Downs given to the city.
Fairfax Street formed by
covering the Frome.

1862
Clifton College opened.

1864
Suspension Bridge opened.
Bath and West Show in the Downs.

Population 183,000. Tramway
system begun. First meeting of the
Bristol School Board. Garibaldi
visits the city. Jewish synagogue in
Park Row opened.
1871

Report on Bristol Charities. Hallé
conducts the first music festival at the
Colston Hall. Cumberland basin lock
opened. Horfield Prison begun. Prince of
Wales opens the racecourse at Knowle.
1873

First trams run from Perry Road to
Redland. Bridewell Court opened.
Floods. Bristol Industrial dwellings in
Jacob's Wells Road opened. Downs
Railway tunnel completed..
1875

1872
New spire of St. Mary Redcliffe
erected. Museum and Library
Queen's Road opened.

1874
Mansion House gift to the city.
Free Libraries Act.
Dean Lane colliery explosion.

1876
Bristol University College founded.
No Popery row. Great fire in Christmas
Street, damage costing £80,000.
Central Library opened.

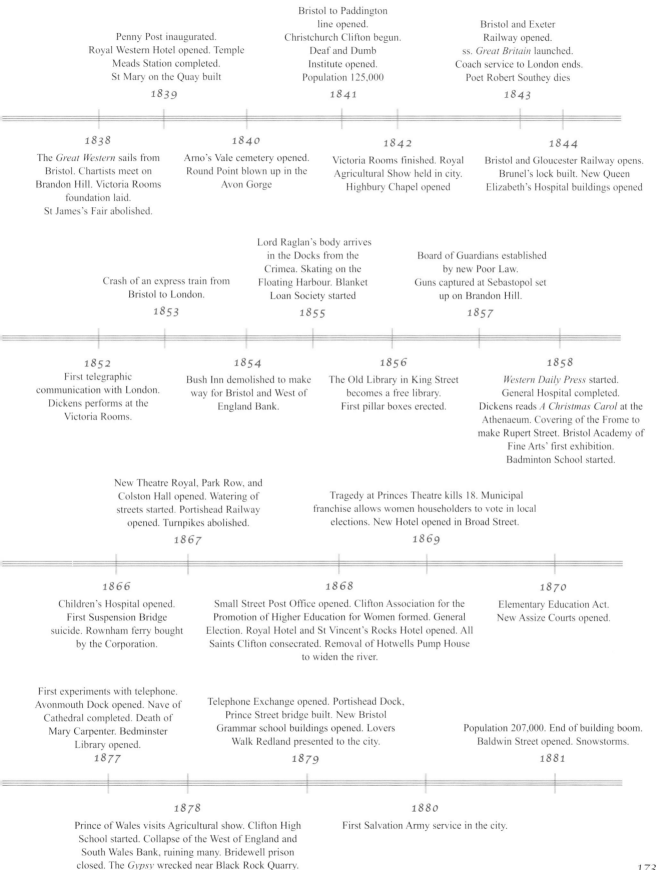

1839
Penny Post inaugurated.
Royal Western Hotel opened. Temple
Meads Station completed.
St Mary on the Quay built

1841
Bristol to Paddington
line opened.
Christchurch Clifton begun.
Deaf and Dumb
Institute opened.
Population 125,000

1843
Bristol and Exeter
Railway opened.
ss. *Great Britain* launched.
Coach service to London ends.
Poet Robert Southey dies

1838
The *Great Western* sails from
Bristol. Chartists meet on
Brandon Hill. Victoria Rooms
foundation laid.
St James's Fair abolished.

1840
Arno's Vale cemetery opened.
Round Point blown up in the
Avon Gorge

1842
Victoria Rooms finished. Royal
Agricultural Show held in city.
Highbury Chapel opened

1844
Bristol and Gloucester Railway opens.
Brunel's lock built. New Queen
Elizabeth's Hospital buildings opened

1853
Crash of an express train from
Bristol to London.

1855
Lord Raglan's body arrives
in the Docks from the
Crimea. Skating on the
Floating Harbour. Blanket
Loan Society started

1857
Board of Guardians established
by new Poor Law.
Guns captured at Sebastopol set
up on Brandon Hill.

1852
First telegraphic
communication with London.
Dickens performs at the
Victoria Rooms.

1854
Bush Inn demolished to make
way for Bristol and West of
England Bank.

1856
The Old Library in King Street
becomes a free library.
First pillar boxes erected.

1858
Western Daily Press started.
General Hospital completed.
Dickens reads *A Christmas Carol* at the
Athenaeum. Covering of the Frome to
make Rupert Street. Bristol Academy of
Fine Arts' first exhibition.
Badminton School started.

1867
New Theatre Royal, Park Row, and
Colston Hall opened. Watering of
streets started. Portishead Railway
opened. Turnpikes abolished.

1869
Tragedy at Princes Theatre kills 18. Municipal
franchise allows women householders to vote in local
elections. New Hotel opened in Broad Street.

1866
Children's Hospital opened.
First Suspension Bridge
suicide. Rownham ferry bought
by the Corporation.

1868
Small Street Post Office opened. Clifton Association for the
Promotion of Higher Education for Women formed. General
Election. Royal Hotel and St Vincent's Rocks Hotel opened. All
Saints Clifton consecrated. Removal of Hotwells Pump House
to widen the river.

1870
Elementary Education Act.
New Assize Courts opened.

1877
First experiments with telephone.
Avonmouth Dock opened. Nave of
Cathedral completed. Death of
Mary Carpenter. Bedminster
Library opened.

1879
Telephone Exchange opened. Portishead Dock,
Prince Street bridge built. New Bristol
Grammar school buildings opened. Lovers
Walk Redland presented to the city.

1881
Population 207,000. End of building boom.
Baldwin Street opened. Snowstorms.

1878
Prince of Wales visits Agricultural show. Clifton High
School started. Collapse of the West of England and
South Wales Bank, ruining many. Bridewell prison
closed. The *Gypsy* wrecked near Black Rock Quarry.

1880
First Salvation Army service in the city.

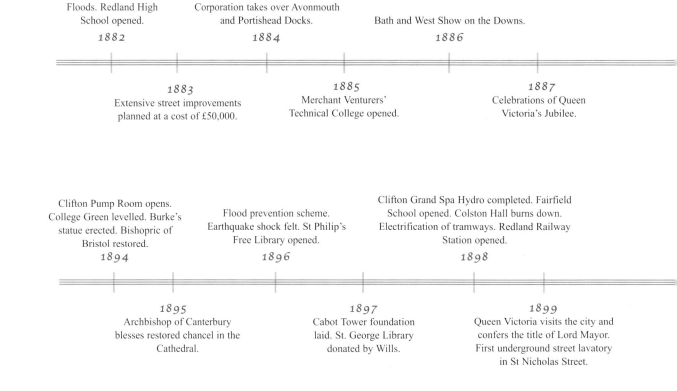

Floods. Redland High
School opened.
1882

Industrial and Fine Art Exhibition.
Corporation takes over Avonmouth
and Portishead Docks.
1884

Bath and West Show on the Downs.
1886

1883
Extensive street improvements
planned at a cost of £50,000.

1885
Merchant Venturers'
Technical College opened.

1887
Celebrations of Queen
Victoria's Jubilee.

Clifton Pump Room opens.
College Green levelled. Burke's
statue erected. Bishopric of
Bristol restored.
1894

Flood prevention scheme.
Earthquake shock felt. St Philip's
Free Library opened.
1896

Clifton Grand Spa Hydro completed. Fairfield
School opened. Colston Hall burns down.
Electrification of tramways. Redland Railway
Station opened.
1898

1895
Archbishop of Canterbury
blesses restored chancel in the
Cathedral.

1897
Cabot Tower foundation
laid. St. George Library
donated by Wills.

1899
Queen Victoria visits the city and
confers the title of Lord Mayor.
First underground street lavatory
in St Nicholas Street.

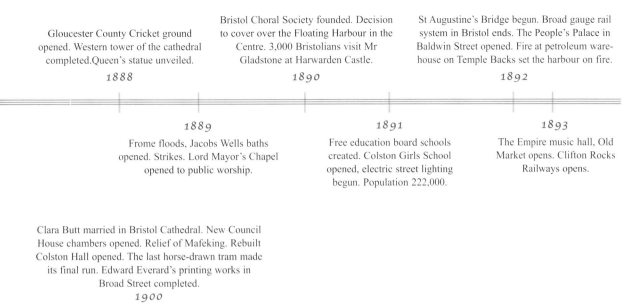

Gloucester County Cricket ground opened. Western tower of the cathedral completed.Queen's statue unveiled.

1888

Bristol Choral Society founded. Decision to cover over the Floating Harbour in the Centre. 3,000 Bristolians visit Mr Gladstone at Harwarden Castle.

1890

St Augustine's Bridge begun. Broad gauge rail system in Bristol ends. The People's Palace in Baldwin Street opened. Fire at petroleum warehouse on Temple Backs set the harbour on fire.

1892

1889

Frome floods, Jacobs Wells baths opened. Strikes. Lord Mayor's Chapel opened to public worship.

1891

Free education board schools created. Colston Girls School opened, electric street lighting begun. Population 222,000.

1893

The Empire music hall, Old Market opens. Clifton Rocks Railways opens.

Clara Butt married in Bristol Cathedral. New Council House chambers opened. Relief of Mafeking. Rebuilt Colston Hall opened. The last horse-drawn tram made its final run. Edward Everard's printing works in Broad Street completed.

1900

1901

Bristol Rifles and Gloucester Volunteers return from service in the Boer War. Population 329,000. Queen Victoria's death.

Acknowledgements

In addition to period newspapers, advertisements, books and directories, the author has referred to, and drawn upon, many sources, some acknowledged in the text, including: the many books about Bristol published by Redcliffe Press; the publications of the Bristol Branch of The Historical Association; *Bristol 1850-1919* David J. Eveleigh, Sutton Publishing; *Industrial History in Pictures: Bristol*, Angus Buchanan and Neil Cossons, David & Charles; *Bristol at Play*, Kathleen Barker, Moonraker Press; *Bristol's Other History*, Bristol Broadsides; *Victorians at Home*, Susan Lasdun, Weidenfeld & Nicholson; *Victorians Unbuttoned*, Sarah Levitt, George Allen & Unwin; *Shops and Shopping: 1800-1914*, Alison Adburgham, George Allen & Unwin.

As ever, Bristol Record Office, Bristol Reference Library and Bristol Museums and Art Gallery have been sources of information and illustration, as have the Clifton College and Reece Winstone Archives.

Many of Redcliffe Press's 180 books about Bristol are still in print.

visit www.redcliffepress.co.uk

write for a catalogue to:
Sales Department
Redcliffe Press Ltd,
81g Pembroke Road,
Bristol. BS8 3EA

email johnsansom@aol.com

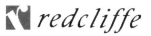